# SRA
# Read to Achieve

### Comprehending
## Narrative Text

D1568847

# Workbook

**Nancy Marchand-Martella**

**Ronald Martella**

Mc
Graw
Hill
Education

## Acknowledgments

NORTHWEST REGIONAL EDUCATIONAL LABORATORY ONLINE
by Northwest Regional Educational Laboratory. Copyright 2008
by Northwest Regional Educational Laboratory. Reproduced with
permission of Northwest Regional Educational Laboratory in the
format Textbook via Copyright Clearance Center.

The authors thank Michael Milone, Ph.D., Assessment Specialist, for
his help in preparing the standardized-test-practice materials.

## Photo Credits

Cover photo: Steven Allen/Brand X Pictures

**MHEonline.com**

Send all inquiries to:
McGraw-Hill Education
8787 Orion Place
Columbus, OH 43240

ISBN: 978-0-07-621998-8
MHID: 0-07-621998-4

Printed in the United States of America.

12 13 14 15 16  QVS  22 21 20 19 18

# Contents

# Contents

**Lesson 1**

Book Title _____

# Character-Analysis Chart

Name _____ Date _____

Main Character: _____

| | **Character Details**<br>(How does the main character look, act, think, or feel because of events or other characters?) | **Personal Connections**<br>(How does the character relate to text, self, world?) |
|---|---|---|
| **Excerpt 1** | | |
| **Excerpt 2** | | |
| **Excerpt 3** | | |
| **Excerpt 4** | | |
| **Excerpt 5** | | |
| **Excerpt 6** | | |
| **Excerpt 7** | | |
| **Excerpt 8** | | |

**Lesson 1**

# Fluency Sample

Name _____ Date _____

Check box: ☐ = Cold Timing   ☐ = Hot Timing

| | Word Count |
|---|---|
| **Overcoming Challenges** | 2 |

| | |
|---|---|
| What do tennis player James Blake, composer Ludwig van Beethoven, | 12 |
| and doctor Elizabeth Blackwell have in common? They triumphed over | 22 |
| difficulties. In fact, many successful people have had to overcome great | 33 |
| odds to make their dreams come true. | 40 |
| When James Blake was five, he began playing tennis with his brother. | 52 |
| At thirteen, Blake was diagnosed with scoliosis. He had to wear a back | 65 |
| brace most of the day for the next five years. In 2004 when he was in his | 82 |
| twenties, Blake slipped on a clay tennis court and broke his neck. Although | 95 |
| he could still walk, his injury almost ended his tennis career. | 106 |
| But Blake did not let this injury stop him. He continued to work toward | 120 |
| becoming one of the best tennis players in the world, and he has succeeded. | 134 |
| Ludwig van Beethoven is recognized as one of the greatest classical-music | 145 |
| composers of all time. In 1796 when he was in his twenties, he noticed he | 160 |
| was having hearing problems. By his mid-forties, Beethoven had become | 170 |
| completely deaf. Yet this disability did not curb Beethoven's love for music. | 182 |
| For years afterward, Beethoven composed music and conducted concerts, | 191 |
| even though he could not hear the music. | 199 |
| In 1849, Elizabeth Blackwell became the first woman to graduate from | 210 |
| medical school in the United States. But the road to becoming a doctor | 223 |
| wasn't an easy one. At that time, many people didn't think women should | 236 |
| be doctors. Blackwell did not let that stop her. | 245 |
| After graduating, Blackwell was not allowed to work in most American | 256 |
| hospitals because she was a woman. She decided to move to France. While | 269 |
| living in France, Blackwell contracted a terrible eye disease. Eventually she | 280 |
| had to have her eye removed. | 286 |
| Again, Blackwell did not let this obstacle stop her. Her continued | 297 |
| medical practice changed the world of medicine. She trained many women | 308 |
| to become nurses and doctors. | 313 |

| | |
|---|---|
| **Total Words Read** | |
| **Total Errors** — | |
| **Correct Words per Minute (CWPM)** = | |

# Unit 1
## No End in Sight

Activity 1

Lesson **2**

Book Title _____

## Setting-Analysis Chart

Name _____ Date _____

| | Setting Details | | Personal Connections |
|---|---|---|---|
| | Where? | When? | (How does this setting relate to text, self, world?) |
| Excerpt 1 | | | |
| Excerpt 2 | | | |
| Excerpt 3 | | | |
| Excerpt 4 | | | |
| Excerpt 5 | | | |
| Excerpt 6 | | | |
| Excerpt 7 | | | |
| Excerpt 8 | | | |

### Lesson 2

# Fluency Practice: Mental Imagery

Name _____ Date _____

## The Feel of Money

Take out some paper money. How much is it worth? You probably find out the value by looking at the bill. Many people are blind or cannot see well enough to read paper money.

In the United States, paper bills are the same size and feel exactly the same. This means that people who are blind cannot tell them apart. They must sometimes ask others to tell them how much money they have or are spending.

Some people who are blind use a machine that tells them how much is printed on the bill. The machine is expensive and must always be carried around.

Not all paper money is like ours. Many other countries make paper money that can be "seen" by people who are blind. For example, the paper money of the European Union is printed in various colors and has large numbers. This makes the bills easier to tell apart.

European bills are also various sizes. For example, a bill worth twenty euros would be larger in size than a bill worth ten euros. Large numbers and varying colors allow someone with poor vision to tell bills apart. A person who is blind can tell the value by feeling the size of each bill.

Some people have asked the United States government to change the way it makes money. They believe that people who are blind should not have to depend on others to help them with their money.

Changing paper money will help people who are blind tell how much each bill is worth. For example, the new bills might have raised printing on them that could be "read" by feeling the bills. The new money could have foil placed in different parts of the bill. Or the new bills could simply be different sizes, like European money.

Possible changes to paper money are still being considered. Don't be surprised if in the future you can tell which bill you are spending without looking at it.

**Directions: Illustrate what you thought about.**

Lesson 3

Book Title _____

# Plot-Analysis Chart

Name _____ Date _____

| | Events (What happened *first*, *next*, *finally*) |
|---|---|
| **Excerpt 1** | |
| **Excerpt 2** | |
| **Excerpt 3** | |
| **Excerpt 4** | |
| **Excerpt 5** | |
| **Excerpt 6** | |
| **Excerpt 7** | |
| **Excerpt 8** | |

| | What was the conflict/problem? | What was the climax/turning point? | What was the resolution/outcome? |
|---|---|---|---|
| | | | |

**Lesson 3**

# Fluency Practice: Standardized Test

Name _____ Date _____

## The Feel of Money

Take out some paper money. How much is it worth? You probably find out the value by looking at the bill. Many people are blind or cannot see well enough to read paper money.

In the United States, paper bills are the same size and feel exactly the same. This means that people who are blind cannot tell them apart. They must sometimes ask others to tell them how much money they have or are spending.

Some people who are blind use a machine that tells them how much is printed on the bill. The machine is expensive and must always be carried around.

Not all paper money is like ours. Many other countries make paper money that can be "seen" by people who are blind. For example, the paper money of the European Union is printed in various colors and has large numbers. This makes the bills easier to tell apart.

European bills are also various sizes. For example, a bill worth twenty euros would be larger in size than a bill worth ten euros. Large numbers and varying colors allow someone with poor vision to tell bills apart. A person who is blind can tell the value by feeling the size of each bill.

Some people have asked the United States government to change the way it makes money. They believe that people who are blind should not have to depend on others to help them with their money.

Changing paper money will help people who are blind tell how much each bill is worth. For example, the new bills might have raised printing on them that could be "read" by feeling the bills. The new money could have foil placed in different parts of the bill. Or the new bills could simply be different sizes, like European money.

Possible changes to paper money are still being considered. Don't be surprised if in the future you can tell which bill you are spending without looking at it.

Score _____ /8 = _____ %

**Directions: Take turns reading the questions. Answer the questions together.**

**Level 1:** "Remember" Questions—each worth 1 point

**For Level 1 questions, fill in the space next to the correct answer in your own Workbook.**

1. Some people who are blind have difficulty telling one U.S. bill from another because
   ○ a. U.S. bills are the same size.
   ○ b. U.S. bills are the same color.
   ○ c. U.S. bills have different textures.
   ○ d. U.S. bills have small print.

**Lesson**
**3**

# Fluency Practice: Standardized Test, continued

Name _____ Date _____

2. Some people who are blind use a machine that tells them the dollar amount printed on a bill. This machine is
   ○ a. too big to carry around.    ○ c. not effective for those who are blind.
   ○ b. expensive to buy.    ○ d. difficult to learn to use.

3. The European Union helps people who are blind by using bills printed
   ○ a. on different textures of paper.
   ○ b. with bar codes on them.
   ○ c. with raised dots.
   ○ d. in various sizes.

4. What is one suggestion from the text for how the United States can change bills?
   ○ a. Print them on different textures of paper.
   ○ b. Put pieces of foil in different parts of the bill.
   ○ c. Print them on different colors of paper.
   ○ d. Put voice-activated bar codes on them.

> **Level 2:** "Understand" Questions—worth 2 points (2 points for correct answer, 1 point for partially correct answer, 0 points for incorrect answer)

**For the Level 2 questions, write the answer in the spaces provided in your own Workbook.**

5. Explain how paper money in the United States may cause problems for those who are blind.

_____

_____

_____

_____

_____

6. Explain some proposed changes to paper bills in the United States.

_____

_____

_____

_____

_____

# Fluency Practice: Information Learned

Name _____ Date _____

## The Feel of Money

Take out some paper money. How much is it worth? You probably find out the value by looking at the bill. Many people are blind or cannot see well enough to read paper money.

In the United States, paper bills are the same size and feel exactly the same. This means that people who are blind cannot tell them apart. They must sometimes ask others to tell them how much money they have or are spending.

Some people who are blind use a machine that tells them how much is printed on the bill. The machine is expensive and must always be carried around.

Not all paper money is like ours. Many other countries make paper money that can be "seen" by people who are blind. For example, the paper money of the European Union is printed in various colors and has large numbers. This makes the bills easier to tell apart.

European bills are also various sizes. For example, a bill worth twenty euros would be larger in size than a bill worth ten euros. Large numbers and varying colors allow someone with poor vision to tell bills apart. A person who is blind can tell the value by feeling the size of each bill.

Some people have asked the United States government to change the way it makes money. They believe that people who are blind should not have to depend on others to help them with their money.

Changing paper money will help people who are blind tell how much each bill is worth. For example, the new bills might have raised printing on them that could be "read" by feeling the bills. The new money could have foil placed in different parts of the bill. Or the new bills could simply be different sizes, like European money.

Possible changes to paper money are still being considered. Don't be surprised if in the future you can tell which bill you are spending without looking at it.

. . . . . . . . . . . . . . . . . . . . . . . . . . . . . . . . . . . . . . . .

**Directions: Write three things you learned after reading the fluency passage.**

1. I learned _____

_____.

2. I learned _____

_____.

3. I learned _____

_____.

**Lesson**
**5**

# Think-Pair-Share

Name _____ Date _____

**Directions**

**Directions: Use the Think-Pair-Share Strategy to complete the question below.**

**Step 1:** **Think** about the question for one minute.

**Step 2:** **Pair,** and complete the question with your partner.

**Step 3:** **Share** what you wrote with the class.

**Apply**

Suppose you're the director for a movie based on the book *No End in Sight*. *Apply* your knowledge of the characters and setting in the book to determine the actors for your movie, which part each will play, and where your movie will be filmed. Defend your answer.

Lesson
2

# Fluency Practice: Mental Imagery

Name _____ Date _____

## The Iditarod

The Iditarod is a race that takes place in Alaska. People come from all over the world to compete in the Iditarod. The race is run by people who drive sleds pulled by dogs. The people who drive the dogsleds are called "mushers." The course is more than 1,150 miles long. It takes a person in this race more than a week to cross the finish line.

The race and the route of the Iditarod are part of Alaska's history. In the 1920s, gold mines were established far from the cities. Supplies had to be taken to the mining towns, and gold had to be brought back to the cities. Sleds and dogs were used to carry these materials back and forth. The trips were difficult and dangerous.

Today the Iditarod follows those same trails. The race starts in Anchorage, a large city. From there, the racers must travel to several checkpoints. The checkpoint locations are different every year. The course runs through icy fields, across frozen rivers, and over large mountains. The winner is the first person to cross the finish line in the city of Nome.

The Iditarod is a bit different from other races. The racers may race and rest whenever they want. Some people may race for long periods, stopping only occasionally to rest, to eat, or to sleep. Other people may stop each night and wait until day to race. The mushers may feed their dogs snacks throughout the trip, or they may give the dogs large meals once or twice a day. Mushers have various strategies for winning the race.

Racers prepare all year long for the race. The people of Alaska pay close attention to the Iditarod. They come out to watch the racers pass by their homes and to cheer the people on. The winner of the Iditarod is considered a hero in Alaska.

**Directions: Illustrate what you thought about.**

**Lesson 3**

# Fluency Practice: Standardized Test

Name _____ Date _____

## The Iditarod

The Iditarod is a race that takes place in Alaska. People come from all over the world to compete in the Iditarod. The race is run by people who drive sleds pulled by dogs. The people who drive the dogsleds are called "mushers." The course is more than 1,150 miles long. It takes a person in this race more than a week to cross the finish line.

The race and the route of the Iditarod are part of Alaska's history. In the 1920s, gold mines were established far from the cities. Supplies had to be taken to the mining towns, and gold had to be brought back to the cities. Sleds and dogs were used to carry these materials back and forth. The trips were difficult and dangerous.

Today the Iditarod follows those same trails. The race starts in Anchorage, a large city. From there, the racers must travel to several checkpoints. The checkpoint locations are different every year. The course runs through icy fields, across frozen rivers, and over large mountains. The winner is the first person to cross the finish line in the city of Nome.

The Iditarod is a bit different from other races. The racers may race and rest whenever they want. Some people may race for long periods, stopping only occasionally to rest, to eat, or to sleep. Other people may stop each night and wait until day to race. The mushers may feed their dogs snacks throughout the trip, or they may give the dogs large meals once or twice a day. Mushers have various strategies for winning the race.

Racers prepare all year long for the race. The people of Alaska pay close attention to the Iditarod. They come out to watch the racers pass by their homes and to cheer the people on. The winner of the Iditarod is considered a hero in Alaska.

• • • • • • • • • • • • • • • • • • • • • • • • • • • • • • • • • • •

Score _____ /8 = _____ %

**Directions: Take turns reading the questions. Answer the questions together.**

**Level 1:** "Remember" Questions—each worth 1 point

**For Level 1 questions, fill in the space next to the correct answer in your own Workbook.**

1. Where does the Iditarod take place?
   ○ a. Antarctica
   ○ b. Norway
   ○ c. Alaska
   ○ d. Iceland

Lesson
**3**

# Fluency Practice: Standardized Test, continued

Name _____ Date _____

**2.** What are the people who drive the dog sleds called?
- ○ a. Jockeys
- ○ b. Riders
- ○ c. Sled drivers
- ○ d. Mushers

**3.** How long does it take someone in the Iditarod to complete the race?
- ○ a. More than a week
- ○ b. Less than a week
- ○ c. More than two weeks
- ○ d. About a month

**4.** How were the Iditarod trails first used in the 1920s?
- ○ a. To transport injured hikers to safety
- ○ b. To take supplies to mining towns and to bring gold back to cities
- ○ c. To train search-and-rescue dogs
- ○ d. To help settlers expand their settlements

> **Level 2:** "Understand" Questions—worth 2 points (2 points for correct answer,
> 1 point for partially correct answer, 0 points for incorrect answer)

**For the Level 2 questions, write the answer in the spaces provided in your own Workbook.**

**5.** Describe the Iditarod course. Include in your response the cities in which the race begins and ends.

_____

_____

_____

_____

**6.** Explain how the Iditarod is different from other races.

_____

_____

_____

_____

_____

_____

**Lesson 4**

Book Title _____

# Story-Components Chart

Name _____ Date _____

**Author(s):**

**Illustrator(s)** (if any):

**Genre:**

☐ Fiction          ☐ Nonfiction

**Theme:**
What is the moral of the story?

**Perspective:**
What is the point of view of the story?

☐ First person     ☐ Second person     ☐ Third person

**Mood:**
How did you feel while you read the story?

**Author's Purpose:**
Why did the author(s) write the story?

☐ To persuade     ☐ To inform     ☐ To entertain

## Lesson 4

# Fluency Practice: Information Learned

Name _____ Date _____

## The Iditarod

The Iditarod is a race that takes place in Alaska. People come from all over the world to compete in the Iditarod. The race is run by people who drive sleds pulled by dogs. The people who drive the dogsleds are called "mushers." The course is more than 1,150 miles long. It takes a person in this race more than a week to cross the finish line.

The race and the route of the Iditarod are part of Alaska's history. In the 1920s, gold mines were established far from the cities. Supplies had to be taken to the mining towns, and gold had to be brought back to the cities. Sleds and dogs were used to carry these materials back and forth. The trips were difficult and dangerous.

Today the Iditarod follows those same trails. The race starts in Anchorage, a large city. From there, the racers must travel to several checkpoints. The checkpoint locations are different every year. The course runs through icy fields, across frozen rivers, and over large mountains. The winner is the first person to cross the finish line in the city of Nome.

The Iditarod is a bit different from other races. The racers may race and rest whenever they want. Some people may race for long periods, stopping only occasionally to rest, to eat, or to sleep. Other people may stop each night and wait until day to race. The mushers may feed their dogs snacks throughout the trip, or they may give the dogs large meals once or twice a day. Mushers have various strategies for winning the race.

Racers prepare all year long for the race. The people of Alaska pay close attention to the Iditarod. They come out to watch the racers pass by their homes and to cheer the people on. The winner of the Iditarod is considered a hero in Alaska.

. . . . . . . . . . . . . . . . . . . . . . . . . . . . . . . . . . . . . .

**Directions: Write three things you learned after reading the fluency passage.**

**1.** I learned _____

_____.

**2.** I learned _____

_____.

**3.** I learned _____

_____.

**Lesson 5**

# Think-Pair-Share

Name _____ Date _____

**Directions:** Use the Think-Pair-Share Strategy to complete the question below.

**Step 1:** **Think** about the question for one minute.

**Step 2:** **Pair,** and complete the question with your partner.

**Step 3:** **Share** what you wrote with the class.

Suppose you've been asked to write a book review for *No End in Sight*. *Apply* your knowledge of the story to write the brief book review. Your review should state whether you liked or disliked the book and three reasons you feel this way.

**Unit 3**
**Trial by Ice**

Activity 1

**Lesson 1**

Book Title _____

# Prediction Chart

Name _____ Date _____

| Part 1: Before you read the book: | |
|---|---|
| **Step 1:** *Preview the book.* | |
| **Step 2:** *Make an initial prediction of what you think the book is about.* | I think this book is about . . . |
| **Step 3:** *Establish your purpose for reading the book.* | My purpose for reading the book is . . . |
| **Step 4:** *Ask yourself what you know about the book's topic.* | I know . . . |

| Part 2: Before and after you read each excerpt: | | |
|---|---|---|
| **Step 1:** *Preview the excerpt.* | **Step 2:** *Make a prediction of what you think the excerpt is about.* | **Step 3:** *Verify your prediction.* |
| **Excerpt 1** | I think today's excerpt is about . . . | My prediction was<br>CORRECT    INCORRECT |
| **Excerpt 2** | I think today's excerpt is about . . . | My prediction was<br>CORRECT    INCORRECT |
| **Excerpt 3** | I think today's excerpt is about . . . | My prediction was<br>CORRECT    INCORRECT |
| **Excerpt 4** | I think today's excerpt is about . . . | My prediction was<br>CORRECT    INCORRECT |
| **Excerpt 5** | I think today's excerpt is about . . . | My prediction was<br>CORRECT    INCORRECT |
| **Excerpt 6** | I think today's excerpt is about . . . | My prediction was<br>CORRECT    INCORRECT |
| **Excerpt 7** | I think today's excerpt is about . . . | My prediction was<br>CORRECT    INCORRECT |
| **Excerpt 8** | I think today's excerpt is about . . . | My prediction was<br>CORRECT    INCORRECT |

| Part 3: After you read the book: | |
|---|---|
| **Step 1:** *Verify your initial prediction.* | My initial prediction was<br>CORRECT            INCORRECT |

Lesson

1

Book Title _____

# Character-Analysis Chart

Name _____ Date _____

Main Character: _____

| | **Character Details** (How does the main character look, act, think, or feel because of events or other characters?) | **Personal Connections** (How does the character relate to text, self, world?) |
|---|---|---|
| | **Excerpt 1** | |
| | **Excerpt 2** | |
| | **Excerpt 3** | |
| | **Excerpt 4** | |
| | **Excerpt 5** | |
| | **Excerpt 6** | |
| | **Excerpt 7** | |
| | **Excerpt 8** | |

Lesson

1

Book Title _____

## Setting-Analysis Chart

Name _____ Date _____

| | Setting Details | | Personal Connections |
|---|---|---|---|
| | Where? | When? | (How does this setting relate to text, self, world?) |
| Excerpt 1 | | | |
| Excerpt 2 | | | |
| Excerpt 3 | | | |
| Excerpt 4 | | | |
| Excerpt 5 | | | |
| Excerpt 6 | | | |
| Excerpt 7 | | | |
| Excerpt 8 | | | |

Book Title _____

# Plot-Analysis Chart

Name _____ Date _____

| | **Events**<br>(What happened *first, next, finally*) |
|---|---|
| **Excerpt 1** | |
| **Excerpt 2** | |
| **Excerpt 3** | |
| **Excerpt 4** | |
| **Excerpt 5** | |
| **Excerpt 6** | |
| **Excerpt 7** | |
| **Excerpt 8** | |

| What was the conflict/problem? | What was the climax/turning point? | What was the resolution/outcome? |
|---|---|---|
| | | |

# Fluency Practice: Mental Imagery

Name _____ Date _____

## Antarctica: Earth's Nature Park

The continent of Antarctica is found at Earth's South Pole. Antarctica is large and covered with snow and ice. No native people live on Antarctica, and the continent has no government. Instead, Antarctica belongs to the entire world and is shared by all countries.

Although Antarctica is covered with snow and ice, the land includes mountains, and many lakes exist under the ice. Seals, whales, and penguins are among the animals that live in, or in the water around, Antarctica. It may surprise you to learn that Antarctica is considered a desert. The land receives very little rain, and the definition of a desert is "a hot or cold place that does not receive much rain." Most of the water in Antarctica is frozen.

In 1959, the countries of the world agreed to share Antarctica. They signed the Antarctic Treaty. This treaty prevents any one country from claiming Antarctica and also protects Antarctica's environment. No country may drill for oil or mine for minerals or other materials. Instead, countries cooperate and allow scientists from all over the world to study Antarctica.

People who visit or work in Antarctica are careful to preserve the environment. Until the Antarctic Treaty was signed, seals and whales in Antarctica were hunted until they almost became extinct. In addition, hunters and fishermen who visited Antarctica left trash and pollution.

Many scientists who live and work in Antarctica stay in small base camps. These scientists are careful not to disturb the environment. Trash and waste are taken away or treated to minimize harm to the environment.

Most of the people who visit Antarctica are tourists who arrive on cruise ships. These tourists want to see the beautiful scenery and animals unique to the continent. The passengers and staff aboard the tour ships are careful not to harm the land and animals while visiting.

**Directions: Illustrate what you thought about.**

**Lesson 3**

# Fluency Practice: Standardized Test

Name _____ Date _____

## Antarctica: Earth's Nature Park

The continent of Antarctica is found at Earth's South Pole. Antarctica is large and covered with snow and ice. No native people live on Antarctica, and the continent has no government. Instead, Antarctica belongs to the entire world and is shared by all countries.

Although Antarctica is covered with snow and ice, the land includes mountains, and many lakes exist under the ice. Seals, whales, and penguins are among the animals that live in, or in the water around, Antarctica. It may surprise you to learn that Antarctica is considered a desert. The land receives very little rain, and the definition of a desert is "a hot or cold place that does not receive much rain." Most of the water in Antarctica is frozen.

In 1959, the countries of the world agreed to share Antarctica. They signed the Antarctic Treaty. This treaty prevents any one country from claiming Antarctica and also protects Antarctica's environment. No country may drill for oil or mine for minerals or other materials. Instead, countries cooperate and allow scientists from all over the world to study Antarctica.

People who visit or work in Antarctica are careful to preserve the environment. Until the Antarctic Treaty was signed, seals and whales in Antarctica were hunted until they almost became extinct. In addition, hunters and fishermen who visited Antarctica left trash and pollution.

Many scientists who live and work in Antarctica stay in small base camps. These scientists are careful not to disturb the environment. Trash and waste are taken away or treated to minimize harm to the environment.

Most of the people who visit Antarctica are tourists who arrive on cruise ships. These tourists want to see the beautiful scenery and animals unique to the continent. The passengers and staff aboard the tour ships are careful not to harm the land and animals while visiting.

Score _____ /8 = _____ %

**Directions: Take turns reading the questions. Answer the questions together.**

**Level 1:** "Remember" Questions—each worth 1 point

**For Level 1 questions, fill in the space next to the correct answer in your own Workbook.**

1. The continent of Antarctica is located
   ○ a. at the South Pole.
   ○ b. along the equator.
   ○ c. at the North Pole.
   ○ d. in the Tropic of Cancer.

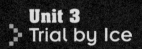

# Fluency Practice: Standardized Test, continued

Name _____ Date _____

2. What types of animals would you find on or in the waters around Antarctica?
   ○ a. Seals, whales, and penguins     ○ c. Parrots, frogs, and panthers
   ○ b. Lions, giraffes, and piranhas   ○ d. Deer, grizzly bears, and trout

3. How is Antarctica described in the selection?
   ○ a. Deciduous forest     ○ c. Grassland
   ○ b. Coniferous forest    ○ d. Desert

4. What did the countries of the world sign in 1959 that allowed them to share and protect Antarctica?
   ○ a. The South Pole Agreement
   ○ b. The Preservation and Protection Act
   ○ c. The Antarctic Treaty
   ○ d. The Hopewell Doctrine

> **Level 2:** "Understand" Questions—worth 2 points (2 points for correct answer,
> 1 point for partially correct answer, 0 points for incorrect answer)

**For the Level 2 questions, write the answer in the spaces provided in your own Workbook.**

5. Explain how the countries of the world are working to protect and preserve Antarctica.

   _____

   _____

   _____

   _____

   _____

   _____

6. Describe Antarctica's environment.

   _____

   _____

   _____

   _____

   _____

## Lesson 4

# Fluency Practice: Information Learned

Name _____ Date _____

## Antarctica: Earth's Nature Park

The continent of Antarctica is found at Earth's South Pole. Antarctica is large and covered with snow and ice. No native people live on Antarctica, and the continent has no government. Instead, Antarctica belongs to the entire world and is shared by all countries.

Although Antarctica is covered with snow and ice, the land includes mountains, and many lakes exist under the ice. Seals, whales, and penguins are among the animals that live in, or in the water around, Antarctica. It may surprise you to learn that Antarctica is considered a desert. The land receives very little rain, and the definition of a desert is "a hot or cold place that does not receive much rain." Most of the water in Antarctica is frozen.

In 1959, the countries of the world agreed to share Antarctica. They signed the Antarctic Treaty. This treaty prevents any one country from claiming Antarctica and also protects Antarctica's environment. No country may drill for oil or mine for minerals or other materials. Instead, countries cooperate and allow scientists from all over the world to study Antarctica.

People who visit or work in Antarctica are careful to preserve the environment. Until the Antarctic Treaty was signed, seals and whales in Antarctica were hunted until they almost became extinct. In addition, hunters and fishermen who visited Antarctica left trash and pollution.

Many scientists who live and work in Antarctica stay in small base camps. These scientists are careful not to disturb the environment. Trash and waste are taken away or treated to minimize harm to the environment.

Most of the people who visit Antarctica are tourists who arrive on cruise ships. These tourists want to see the beautiful scenery and animals unique to the continent. The passengers and staff aboard the tour ships are careful not to harm the land and animals while visiting.

· · · · · · · · · · · · · · · · · · · · · · · · · · · · · · · · · · · ·

**Directions: Write three things you learned after reading the fluency passage.**

**1.** I learned _____

_____.

**2.** I learned _____

_____.

**3.** I learned _____

_____.

## Think-Pair-Share

Name _____ Date _____

**Directions: Use the Think-Pair-Share Strategy to complete the question below.**

**Step 1: Think** about the question for one minute.

**Step 2: Pair,** and complete the question with your partner.

**Step 3: Share** what you wrote with the class.

. . . . . . . . . . . . . . . . . . . . . . . . . . . . . . . . . . . . . . . . . .

Suppose you're a director for a movie based on the book *Trial by Ice. Apply* your knowledge of the characters and setting in the book to determine who should star in your movie, which part each will play, and where your movie will be filmed. Defend your answer.

Lesson

1

Book Title _____

# Question-Generation Chart

Name _____ Date _____

| Part 1: Generate literal questions. | Part 2: Generate inferential questions. |
|---|---|
| *Write one of the following questions and its answer.* | *Write one of the following questions and its answer.* |
| Who _____? What _____? | How do you think _____ felt when _____? |
| Where _____? When _____? | Why would _____ act the way he/she/they acted? |
| Why _____? How _____? | How would the story have changed if _____? |
| Other literal questions: _____ | Other inferential questions: _____ |
| **Excerpt 1** | |
| **Excerpt 2** | |
| **Excerpt 3** | |
| **Excerpt 4** | |
| **Excerpt 5** | |
| **Excerpt 6** | |
| **Excerpt 7** | |
| **Excerpt 8** | |

**Lesson 2**

# Fluency Practice: Mental Imagery

Name _____ Date _____

## The Age of Exploration

One of the greatest periods of world exploration occurred between the fifteenth and seventeenth centuries. This period is called the Age of Exploration. During this time, explorers from Europe made many discoveries around the world.

The main purpose for exploring during this time was to find and trade goods. Europeans needed spices, silk, and other products found in Africa and Asia, but traveling to distant places took long periods of time. It was important to find good trade routes that were both safe from thieves and short.

The Age of Exploration began in Portugal as explorers launched ships in search of a better route to Africa. Up to this time, most traders made long, difficult trips across the desert. Prince Henry the Navigator was the leader of exploration for Portugal in the 1400s. He had great success finding trade routes to Africa across the ocean.

After Prince Henry discovered these routes, other explorers began to find other routes as well. Soon explorers were traveling to India to trade. To compete with Portugal's India trading routes, Spain gave explorers—such as Christopher Columbus—ships so they could find better routes to India. In his quest to find these routes, Columbus instead found the continent of North America.

Explorers from other countries began visiting North America in the 1500s. Spain began to colonize the new world. Hernán Cortés settled in Mexico. Juan Ponce de León searched for the legendary Fountain of Youth. His travels resulted in the discovery of Florida, which was then quickly colonized.

The success of explorers from Spain and Portugal led France and England to send ships to America. The explorers from these two countries claimed land and often fought over territory, taking land from each other by force. Several wars were waged for territory. Finally came the American Revolution, leading to the creation of a new nation independent from European countries. The end of the American Revolution also marked the end of the Age of Exploration.

**Directions: Illustrate what you thought about.**

**Lesson 3**

# Fluency Practice: Standardized Test

Name _____ Date _____

## The Age of Exploration

One of the greatest periods of world exploration occurred between the fifteenth and seventeenth centuries. This period is called the Age of Exploration. During this time, explorers from Europe made many discoveries around the world.

The main purpose for exploring during this time was to find and trade goods. Europeans needed spices, silk, and other products found in Africa and Asia, but traveling to distant places took long periods of time. It was important to find good trade routes that were both safe from thieves and short.

The Age of Exploration began in Portugal as explorers launched ships in search of a better route to Africa. Up to this time, most traders made long, difficult trips across the desert. Prince Henry the Navigator was the leader of exploration for Portugal in the 1400s. He had great success finding trade routes to Africa across the ocean.

After Prince Henry discovered these routes, other explorers began to find other routes as well. Soon explorers were traveling to India

to trade. To compete with Portugal's India trading routes, Spain gave explorers—such as Christopher Columbus—ships so they could find better routes to India. In his quest to find these routes, Columbus instead found the continent of North America.

Explorers from other countries began visiting North America in the 1500s. Spain began to colonize the new world. Hernán Cortés settled in Mexico. Juan Ponce de León searched for the legendary Fountain of Youth. His travels resulted in the discovery of Florida, which was then quickly colonized.

The success of explorers from Spain and Portugal led France and England to send ships to America. The explorers from these two countries claimed land and often fought over territory, taking land from each other by force. Several wars were waged for territory. Finally came the American Revolution, leading to the creation of a new nation independent from European countries. The end of the American Revolution also marked the end of the Age of Exploration.

Score _____ /8 = _____ %

**Directions: Take turns reading the questions. Answer the questions together.**

| Level 1: "Remember" Questions—each worth 1 point |

**For Level 1 questions, fill in the space next to the correct answer in your own Workbook.**

1. What term describes the time period between the fifteenth and seventeenth centuries?
   ○ a. The Middle Ages
   ○ b. The Age of Exploration
   ○ c. The Industrial Revolution
   ○ d. The Age of Discovery

**Lesson 3**

# Fluency Practice: Standardized Test, continued

Name _____ Date _____

**2.** A good trade route is one that
- ○ a. is short and safe from thieves.
- ○ b. is shared with other countries.
- ○ c. is near the coast of Africa.
- ○ d. is found by accident.

**3.** For what country did Prince Henry the Navigator lead his exploration?
- ○ a. Portugal
- ○ b. India
- ○ c. Spain
- ○ d. Africa

**4.** What explorer found the continent of North America in search of better routes to India?
- ○ a. James Cook
- ○ b. Ferdinand Magellan
- ○ c. John Cabot
- ○ d. Christopher Columbus

> **Level 2:** "Understand" Questions—worth 2 points (2 points for correct answer, 1 point for partially correct answer, 0 points for incorrect answer)

**For the Level 2 questions, write the answers in the space provided in your own Workbook.**

**5.** Explain what happened in North America after European explorers arrived there.

_____

_____

_____

_____

_____

_____

**6.** Explain how the success of Spain and Portugal's exploration affected France's and England's explorations.

_____

_____

_____

_____

_____

_____

Lesson
4

Book Title _____

# Story-Components Chart

Name _____ Date _____

| Author(s): |
|---|
| **Illustrator(s)** (if any): |
| **Genre:**<br><br>☐ Fiction     ☐ Nonfiction |
| **Theme:**<br>What is the moral of the story? |
| **Perspective:**<br>What is the point of view of the story?<br><br>☐ First person     ☐ Second person     ☐ Third person |
| **Mood:**<br>How did you feel while you read the story? |
| **Author's Purpose:**<br>Why did the author(s) write the story?<br><br>☐ To persuade     ☐ To inform     ☐ To entertain |

## Lesson 4

# Fluency Practice: Information Learned

Name _____ Date _____

## The Age of Exploration

One of the greatest periods of world exploration occurred between the fifteenth and seventeenth centuries. This period is called the Age of Exploration. During this time, explorers from Europe made many discoveries around the world.

The main purpose for exploring during this time was to find and trade goods. Europeans needed spices, silk, and other products found in Africa and Asia, but traveling to distant places took long periods of time. It was important to find good trade routes that were both safe from thieves and short.

The Age of Exploration began in Portugal as explorers launched ships in search of a better route to Africa. Up to this time, most traders made long, difficult trips across the desert. Prince Henry the Navigator was the leader of exploration for Portugal in the 1400s. He had great success finding trade routes to Africa across the ocean.

After Prince Henry discovered these routes, other explorers began to find other routes as well. Soon explorers were traveling to India to trade. To compete with Portugal's India trading routes, Spain gave explorers—such as Christopher Columbus—ships so they could find better routes to India. In his quest to find these routes, Columbus instead found the continent of North America.

Explorers from other countries began visiting North America in the 1500s. Spain began to colonize the new world. Hernán Cortés settled in Mexico. Juan Ponce de León searched for the legendary Fountain of Youth. His travels resulted in the discovery of Florida, which was then quickly colonized.

The success of explorers from Spain and Portugal led France and England to send ships to America. The explorers from these two countries claimed land and often fought over territory, taking land from each other by force. Several wars were waged for territory. Finally came the American Revolution, leading to the creation of a new nation independent from European countries. The end of the American Revolution also marked the end of the Age of Exploration.

**Directions: Write three things you learned after reading the fluency passage.**

**1.** I learned _____

_____.

**2.** I learned _____

_____.

**3.** I learned _____

_____.

## Think-Pair-Share

Name _____ Date _____

**Directions: Use the Think-Pair-Share Strategy to complete the question below.**

**Step 1:** **Think** about the question for one minute.

**Step 2:** **Pair,** and complete the question with your partner.

**Step 3:** **Share** what you wrote with the class.

- - - - - - - - - - - - - - - - - - - - - - - - - - - - - - - - - - - - - - - - - - - - - - - - - - -

Suppose you've been asked to write a book review for *Trial by Ice. Apply* your knowledge of the story to write the brief book review. Your review should state whether you liked or disliked the book and three reasons you feel this way. Which book did you like better—*No End in Sight* or *Trial by Ice?* Why?

# Unit 5
## Princess of the Press

**Activity 1**

## Lesson 1

Book Title _____

# Prediction Chart

Name _____ Date _____

| Part 1: Before you read the book: | |
|---|---|
| **Step 1:** *Preview the book.* | |
| **Step 2:** *Make an initial prediction of what you think the book is about.* | I think this book is about . . . |
| **Step 3:** *Establish your purpose for reading the book.* | My purpose for reading the book is . . . |
| **Step 4:** *Ask yourself what you know about the book's topic.* | I know . . . |

| Part 2: Before and after you read each excerpt: | | |
|---|---|---|
| **Step 1:** *Preview the excerpt.* | **Step 2:** *Make a prediction of what you think the excerpt is about.* | **Step 3:** *Verify your prediction.* |
| **Excerpt 1** | I think today's excerpt is about . . . | My prediction was<br>CORRECT    INCORRECT |
| **Excerpt 2** | I think today's excerpt is about . . . | My prediction was<br>CORRECT    INCORRECT |
| **Excerpt 3** | I think today's excerpt is about . . . | My prediction was<br>CORRECT    INCORRECT |
| **Excerpt 4** | I think today's excerpt is about . . . | My prediction was<br>CORRECT    INCORRECT |
| **Excerpt 5** | I think today's excerpt is about . . . | My prediction was<br>CORRECT    INCORRECT |
| **Excerpt 6** | I think today's excerpt is about . . . | My prediction was<br>CORRECT    INCORRECT |
| **Excerpt 7** | I think today's excerpt is about . . . | My prediction was<br>CORRECT    INCORRECT |
| **Excerpt 8** | I think today's excerpt is about . . . | My prediction was<br>CORRECT    INCORRECT |

| Part 3: After you read the book: | |
|---|---|
| **Step 1:** *Verify your initial prediction.* | My initial prediction was<br>CORRECT                    INCORRECT |

**Lesson 1**

Book Title _____

# Question-Generation Chart

Name _____ Date _____

| Part 1: Generate literal questions. | Part 2: Generate inferential questions. |
|---|---|
| *Write one of the following questions and its answer.*<br>Who _____? What _____?<br>Where _____? When _____?<br>Why _____? How _____?<br>Other literal questions: _____ | *Write one of the following questions and its answer.*<br>How do you think _____ felt when _____?<br>Why would _____ act the way he/she/they acted?<br>How would the story have changed if _____?<br>Other inferential questions: _____ |
| **Excerpt 1** | |
| **Excerpt 2** | |
| **Excerpt 3** | |
| **Excerpt 4** | |
| **Excerpt 5** | |
| **Excerpt 6** | |
| **Excerpt 7** | |
| **Excerpt 8** | |

Lesson 1

Book Title _____

## Clarification Chart

Name _____ Date _____

| Part 1: Reread and adjust reading rate. | |
|---|---|
| **Part 2: Decode multipart words.** | **Part 3: Use word-learning strategies.** |
| | Step 1: Use context clues. |
| | Step 2: Use a glossary. |
| | Step 3: Use a dictionary or an online dictionary. |
| Excerpt 1 | |
| Excerpt 2 | |
| Excerpt 3 | |
| Excerpt 4 | |
| Excerpt 5 | |
| Excerpt 6 | |
| Excerpt 7 | |
| Excerpt 8 | |

**Lesson**
**1**

Book Title _____

# Character-Analysis Chart

Name _____ Date _____

Main Character: _____

| | **Character Details** (How does the main character look, act, think, or feel as a result of events or other characters?) | **Personal Connections** (How does the character relate to text, self, world?) |
|---|---|---|
| | Excerpt 1 | |
| | Excerpt 2 | |
| | Excerpt 3 | |
| | Excerpt 4 | |
| | Excerpt 5 | |
| | Excerpt 6 | |
| | Excerpt 7 | |
| | Excerpt 8 | |

Book Title _____

# Setting-Analysis Chart

Name _____ Date _____

| | Setting Details | | Personal Connections |
| --- | --- | --- | --- |
| | Where? | When? | (How does this setting relate to text, self, world?) |
| Excerpt 1 | | | |
| Excerpt 2 | | | |
| Excerpt 3 | | | |
| Excerpt 4 | | | |
| Excerpt 5 | | | |
| Excerpt 6 | | | |
| Excerpt 7 | | | |
| Excerpt 8 | | | |

Lesson
1

Book Title _____

# Plot-Analysis Chart

Name _____ Date _____

| | **Events**<br>(What happened *first*, *next*, *finally*) |
|---|---|
| **Excerpt 1** | |
| **Excerpt 2** | |
| **Excerpt 3** | |
| **Excerpt 4** | |
| **Excerpt 5** | |
| **Excerpt 6** | |
| **Excerpt 7** | |
| **Excerpt 8** | |

| What was the conflict/problem? | What was the climax/turning point? | What was the resolution/outcome? |
|---|---|---|
| | | |

**Lesson 2**

# Fluency Practice: Mental Imagery

Name _____ Date _____

## The Civil Rights Act of 1964

During the 1950s, the movement for civil rights in the United States began to escalate. In 1960, John F. Kennedy was elected president. Two years after his election, Kennedy proposed a Civil Rights Act. This legislation stated that all people would be guaranteed equal access to public places. This meant African Americans could go into restaurants, theaters, schools, and other places they previously were forbidden to enter.

The proposed Civil Rights legislation would also require employers to give equal opportunity to all people. This meant companies would have to consider every job applicant equally—black, white, male, or female.

Finally, the act outlawed unequal voter registration rules. At this time, some states made it difficult for African Americans to vote. Some local governments made special rules. These rules often made it difficult for minorities to prove they were eligible to vote. Under this legislation, these rules would no longer be allowed.

In order to enforce these rules, the Civil Rights Act included giving the government the power to punish anyone who violated the act. Businesses or organizations that violated the Civil Rights Act could be made to pay large fines.

Kennedy died soon after proposing the Civil Rights Act. His successor, President Lyndon Johnson, worked hard to make sure the Civil Rights Act was passed. This passage became a huge battle for many reasons. Some members of Congress tried to stop the passage by not letting Congress vote on it. However, Johnson's efforts paid off in the end. He gained the support of several leaders in the Senate who agreed with the passage and what it would mean to all people in the United States. On July 2, 1964, the act was finally passed and was signed by Johnson in a special ceremony. Today, this act guarantees the rights of all people, regardless of their race or gender.

**Directions: Illustrate what you thought about.**

# Fluency Practice: Standardized Test

Name _____ Date _____

## The Civil Rights Act of 1964

During the 1950s, the movement for civil rights in the United States began to escalate. In 1960, John F. Kennedy was elected president. Two years after his election, Kennedy proposed a Civil Rights Act. This legislation stated that all people would be guaranteed equal access to public places. This meant African Americans could go into restaurants, theaters, schools, and other places they previously were forbidden to enter.

The proposed Civil Rights legislation would also require employers to give equal opportunity to all people. This meant companies would have to consider every job applicant equally— black, white, male, or female.

Finally, the act outlawed unequal voter registration rules. At this time, some states made it difficult for African Americans to vote. Some local governments made special rules. These rules often made it difficult for minorities to prove they were eligible to vote. Under this legislation, these rules would no longer be allowed.

In order to enforce these rules, the Civil Rights Act included giving the government the power to punish anyone who violated the act. Businesses or organizations that violated the Civil Rights Act could be made to pay large fines.

Kennedy died soon after proposing the Civil Rights Act. His successor, President Lyndon Johnson, worked hard to make sure the Civil Rights Act was passed. This passage became a huge battle for many reasons. Some members of Congress tried to stop the passage by not letting Congress vote on it. However, Johnson's efforts paid off in the end. He gained the support of several leaders in the Senate who agreed with the passage and what it would mean to all people in the United States. On July 2, 1964, the act was finally passed and was signed by Johnson in a special ceremony. Today, this act guarantees the rights of all people, regardless of their race or gender.

Score _____ /8 = _____ %

**Directions: Take turns reading the questions. Answer the questions together.**

**Level 1:** "Remember" Questions—each worth 1 point

**For Level 1 questions, fill in the space next to the correct answer in your own Workbook.**

1. What president proposed the Civil Rights Act?
   - a. Richard Nixon
   - b. Gerald Ford
   - c. John F. Kennedy
   - d. Franklin Roosevelt

## Lesson 3

# Fluency Practice: Standardized Test, continued

Name _____ Date _____

2. What did "equal opportunity" do for civil rights in America?
   ○ a. Made it easier for immigrants to become American citizens.
   ○ b. Required companies to consider every job applicant equally—black, white, male, or female.
   ○ c. Required states to provide an equal education for all children with disabilities.
   ○ d. Gave women the right to vote.

3. Before the Civil Rights Act, how did some parts of the country make it difficult for African Americans to vote?
   ○ a. Some local governments required minorities to own land and a house to vote.
   ○ b. Some local governments required minorities to pass voting tests.
   ○ c. Some local governments made it difficult for minorities to prove they were eligible to vote.
   ○ d. Some local governments passed laws to stop minorities from voting.

4. Today, the Civil Rights Act ensures
   ○ a. basic rights for all people, regardless of their race or gender.
   ○ b. enough food for all people during periods of economic crisis in America.
   ○ c. Native Americans receive payment for tribal land taken by force.
   ○ d. all homeless people are provided homes.

> **Level 2:** "Understand" Questions—worth 2 points (2 points for correct answer, 1 point for partially correct answer, 0 points for incorrect answer)

**For the Level 2 questions, write the answer in the spaces provided in your own Workbook.**

5. Explain how the Civil Rights Act was enforced.

   _____

   _____

   _____

6. Explain how passing the Civil Rights Act through Congress turned into a "battle."

   _____

   _____

   _____

   _____

**Lesson 4**

# Fluency Practice: Information Learned

Name _____ Date _____

## The Civil Rights Act of 1964

During the 1950s, the movement for civil rights in the United States began to escalate. In 1960, John F. Kennedy was elected president. Two years after his election, Kennedy proposed a Civil Rights Act. This legislation stated that all people would be guaranteed equal access to public places. This meant African Americans could go into restaurants, theaters, schools, and other places they previously were forbidden to enter.

The proposed Civil Rights legislation would also require employers to give equal opportunity to all people. This meant companies would have to consider every job applicant equally— black, white, male, or female.

Finally, the act outlawed unequal voter registration rules. At this time, some states made it difficult for African Americans to vote. Some local governments made special rules. These rules often made it difficult for minorities to prove they were eligible to vote. Under this legislation, these rules would no longer be allowed.

In order to enforce these rules, the Civil Rights Act included giving the government the power to punish anyone who violated the act. Businesses or organizations that violated the Civil Rights Act could be made to pay large fines.

Kennedy died soon after proposing the Civil Rights Act. His successor, President Lyndon Johnson, worked hard to make sure the Civil Rights Act was passed. This passage became a huge battle for many reasons. Some members of Congress tried to stop the passage by not letting Congress vote on it. However, Johnson's efforts paid off in the end. He gained the support of several leaders in the Senate who agreed with the passage and what it would mean to all people in the United States. On July 2, 1964, the act was finally passed and was signed by Johnson in a special ceremony. Today, this act guarantees the rights of all people, regardless of their race or gender.

• • • • • • • • • • • • • • • • • • • • • • • • • • • • • • • • • • • • • • • •

**Directions: Write three things you learned after reading the fluency passage.**

**1.** I learned _____

_____.

**2.** I learned _____

_____.

**3.** I learned _____

_____.

## Lesson 5

# Think-Pair-Share

Name _____ Date _____

### Directions

**Use the Think-Pair-Share Strategy to complete the question below.**

**Step 1:** **Think** about the question for one minute.

**Step 2:** **Pair,** and complete the question with your partner.

**Step 3:** **Share** what you wrote with the class.

### Analyze

Suppose you're a newspaper reporter asked to interview Ida B. Wells-Barnett. *Analyze* her experiences in *Princess of the Press* to generate two questions you could ask her. Provide answers to your questions as if Ida B. Wells-Barnett were talking.

**Lesson**
**1**

Book Title _____

# Summarization Chart

Name _____ Date _____

| | Part 1: Retell what happened. | | |
|---|---|---|---|
| | *(First, next, then . . . , finally)* | | |
| | **Part 2: Develop a gist.** | | |
| | **Step 1:** Whom or what the excerpt was about. | **Step 2:** The most important thing about the whom or what. | **Step 3:** The main idea in twenty words or fewer. (Begin with *This excerpt is about . . . .*) |
| | Excerpt 1 | | |
| | Excerpt 2 | | |
| | Excerpt 3 | | |
| | Excerpt 4 | | |

## Lesson 1

# **Summarization Chart,** continued

Name _____ Date _____

| | | |
|---|---|---|
| **Excerpt 5** | | _____ _____ _____ _____ _____ <br> _____ _____ _____ _____ _____ <br> _____ _____ _____ _____ _____ <br> _____ _____ _____ _____ _____ . |
| **Excerpt 6** | | _____ _____ _____ _____ _____ <br> _____ _____ _____ _____ _____ <br> _____ _____ _____ _____ _____ <br> _____ _____ _____ _____ _____ . |
| **Excerpt 7** | | _____ _____ _____ _____ _____ <br> _____ _____ _____ _____ _____ <br> _____ _____ _____ _____ _____ <br> _____ _____ _____ _____ _____ . |
| **Excerpt 8** | | _____ _____ _____ _____ _____ <br> _____ _____ _____ _____ _____ <br> _____ _____ _____ _____ _____ <br> _____ _____ _____ _____ _____ . |
| What was the conflict/problem? | What was the climax/turning point? | What was the resolution/outcome? |
| | | |

## Unit 6
## Princess of the Press

Activity 1

### Lesson 2

# Fluency Practice: Mental Imagery

Name _____ Date _____

## Frederick Douglass

Frederick Douglass is one of the great civil rights leaders in American history. Douglass was born a slave but used education as a tool to better himself and improve the status of many other slaves.

When Douglass was young and a slave, the slaveholder's wife began to teach him to read at the same time she taught her own son to read. Her husband put a stop to the teaching. He reasoned that if slaves learned to read and write, the slaves would use these abilities to become free. Douglass never forgot this, and from that point on, he worked secretly to learn to read and write.

Reading exposed Douglass to new ideas and opinions. He read all the books and newspapers he could find. He also helped other slaves learn to read, risking punishment. Eventually, Douglass escaped and gained his freedom, devoting himself to writing and speaking out against slavery. He told everyone his story and urged people to abandon slavery and grant full rights to slaves.

Douglass believed education was the key to freedom. For this reason, he wanted schools to admit black children. He became a recognized leader for civil rights. During the Civil War, he served as an adviser to President Abraham Lincoln. Douglass told the president that blacks must be free to fight as soldiers in the war. At his urging, Lincoln freed all the slaves in certain states.

After the Civil War, Douglass devoted his efforts to helping blacks get the right to vote. He helped elect Ulysses Grant president. In return, Grant pushed for the Fifteenth Amendment, which guaranteed that black men could vote in every state.

Douglass continued to speak out for civil rights the rest of his life. During his travels, he often encountered examples of discrimination, and he would respond by writing letters to the newspaper, pointing out these examples and calling for change. His story inspired many people to take a stand for civil rights and illustrated the value of education for all people in the United States.

**Directions: Illustrate what you thought about.**

# Fluency Practice: Standardized Test

Name _____ Date _____

## Frederick Douglass

Frederick Douglass is one of the great civil rights leaders in American history. Douglass was born a slave but used education as a tool to better himself and improve the status of many other slaves.

When Douglass was young and a slave, the slaveholder's wife began to teach him to read at the same time she taught her own son to read. Her husband put a stop to the teaching. He reasoned that if slaves learned to read and write, the slaves would use these abilities to become free. Douglass never forgot this, and from that point on, he worked secretly to learn to read and write.

Reading exposed Douglass to new ideas and opinions. He read all the books and newspapers he could find. He also helped other slaves learn to read, risking punishment. Eventually, Douglass escaped and gained his freedom, devoting himself to writing and speaking out against slavery. He told everyone his story and urged people to abandon slavery and grant full rights to slaves.

Douglass believed education was the key to freedom. For this reason, he wanted schools to admit black children. He became a recognized leader for civil rights. During the Civil War, he served as an adviser to President Abraham Lincoln. Douglass told the president that blacks must be free to fight as soldiers in the war. At his urging, Lincoln freed all the slaves in certain states.

After the Civil War, Douglass devoted his efforts to helping blacks get the right to vote. He helped elect Ulysses Grant president. In return, Grant pushed for the Fifteenth Amendment, which guaranteed that black men could vote in every state.

Douglass continued to speak out for civil rights the rest of his life. During his travels, he often encountered examples of discrimination, and he would respond by writing letters to the newspaper, pointing out these examples and calling for change. His story inspired many people to take a stand for civil rights and illustrated the value of education for all people in the United States.

Score _____ /8 = _____ %

**Directions: Take turns reading the questions. Answer the questions together.**

**Level 1:** "Remember" Questions—each worth 1 point

**For Level 1 questions, fill in the space next to the correct answer in your own Workbook.**

1. What did Frederick Douglass use as a tool to better himself and to improve the status of many other slaves?
   - ○ a. Money
   - ○ b. Education
   - ○ c. Friendship
   - ○ d. Social status

**Lesson 3**

# Fluency Practice: Standardized Test, continued

Name _____ Date _____

2. Who began to teach Douglass to read as a young slave?
   - ○ a. His slaveholder's wife
   - ○ b. His schoolteacher
   - ○ c. His father
   - ○ d. His best friend

3. Why did Douglass have to stop learning how to read?
   - ○ a. He ran away from his master before he had time to learn to read well.
   - ○ b. His slaveholder thought if slaves learned how to read and write, they would use those abilities to become free.
   - ○ c. His mother didn't want him to learn how to read out of fear of punishment from the slaveholder.
   - ○ d. His slaveholder kept him so busy working he didn't have time to continue learning how to read.

4. Which president freed the slaves in certain states because of Douglass's urging?
   - ○ a. George Washington
   - ○ b. Grover Cleveland
   - ○ c. Ulysses Grant
   - ○ d. Abraham Lincoln

> **Level 2:** "Understand" Questions—worth 2 points (2 points for correct answer, 1 point for partially correct answer, 0 points for incorrect answer)

**For the Level 2 questions, write the answer in the spaces provided in your own Workbook.**

5. Explain how Frederick Douglass helped African Americans get the right to vote.

_____

_____

_____

_____

_____

6. Explain how Frederick Douglass influenced big changes in civil rights during his lifetime.

_____

_____

_____

_____

_____

Lesson
**4**

Book Title _____

# Story-Components Chart

Name _____ Date _____

| |
|---|
| **Author(s):** |
| |
| **Illustrator(s)** (if any): |
| |
| **Genre:** <br> ☐ Fiction          ☐ Nonfiction |
| **Theme:** <br> What is the moral of the story? |
| |
| **Perspective:** <br> What is the point of view of the story? <br><br> ☐ First person     ☐ Second person     ☐ Third person |
| **Mood:** <br> How did you feel while you read the story? |
| |
| **Author's Purpose:** <br> Why did the author(s) write the story? <br><br> ☐ To persuade     ☐ To inform     ☐ To entertain |

## Lesson 4

# Fluency Practice: Information Learned

Name _____ Date _____

## Frederick Douglass

Frederick Douglass is one of the great civil rights leaders in American history. Douglass was born a slave but used education as a tool to better himself and improve the status of many other slaves.

When Douglass was young and a slave, the slaveholder's wife began to teach him to read at the same time she taught her own son to read. Her husband put a stop to the teaching. He reasoned that if slaves learned to read and write, the slaves would use these abilities to become free. Douglass never forgot this, and from that point on, he worked secretly to learn to read and write.

Reading exposed Douglass to new ideas and opinions. He read all the books and newspapers he could find. He also helped other slaves learn to read, risking punishment. Eventually, Douglass escaped and gained his freedom, devoting himself to writing and speaking out against slavery. He told everyone his story and urged people to abandon slavery and grant full rights to slaves.

Douglass believed education was the key to freedom. For this reason, he wanted schools to admit black children. He became a recognized leader for civil rights. During the Civil War, he served as an adviser to President Abraham Lincoln. Douglass told the president that blacks must be free to fight as soldiers in the war. At his urging, Lincoln freed all the slaves in certain states.

After the Civil War, Douglass devoted his efforts to helping blacks get the right to vote. He helped elect Ulysses Grant president. In return, Grant pushed for the Fifteenth Amendment, which guaranteed that black men could vote in every state.

Douglass continued to speak out for civil rights the rest of his life. During his travels, he often encountered examples of discrimination, and he would respond by writing letters to the newspaper, pointing out these examples and calling for change. His story inspired many people to take a stand for civil rights and illustrated the value of education for all people in the United States.

• • • • • • • • • • • • • • • • • • • • • • • • • • • • • • • • • • • • • • • • •

**Directions: Write three things you learned after reading the fluency passage.**

**1.** I learned _____

_____.

**2.** I learned _____

_____.

**3.** I learned _____

_____.

Lesson
**5**

# Think-Pair-Share

Name _____ Date _____

**Directions: Use the Think-Pair-Share Strategy to complete the question below.**

**Step 1: Think** about the question for one minute.

**Step 2: Pair,** and complete the question with your partner.

**Step 3: Share** what you wrote with the class.

- - - - - - - - - - - - - - - - - - - - - - - - - - - - - - - - - - - - - - - - - - - - -

**Analyze**

Suppose you're a psychologist studying people who have overcome challenges in their lives. *Analyze* what challenges Ida B. Wells-Barnett experienced and how she overcame those challenges. What do Ida B. Wells-Barnett, Rachael Scdoris, and Ernest Shackleton have in common? Explain.

**Unit 7**
**Phineas Gage**

Activity 1

**Lesson 1**

Book Title _____

# Prediction Chart

Name _____ Date _____

| Part 1: Before you read the book: | |
|---|---|
| Step 1: *Preview the book.* | |
| Step 2: *Make an initial prediction of what you think the book is about.* | I think this book is about . . . |
| Step 3: *Establish your purpose for reading the book.* | My purpose for reading the book is . . . |
| Step 4: *Ask yourself what you know about the book's topic.* | I know . . . |

| Part 2: Before and after you read each excerpt: | | |
|---|---|---|
| Step 1: *Preview the excerpt.* | Step 2: *Make a prediction of what you think the excerpt is about.* | Step 3: *Verify your prediction.* |
| Excerpt 1 | I think today's excerpt is about . . . | My prediction was<br>CORRECT  INCORRECT |
| Excerpt 2 | I think today's excerpt is about . . . | My prediction was<br>CORRECT  INCORRECT |
| Excerpt 3 | I think today's excerpt is about . . . | My prediction was<br>CORRECT  INCORRECT |
| Excerpt 4 | I think today's excerpt is about . . . | My prediction was<br>CORRECT  INCORRECT |
| Excerpt 5 | I think today's excerpt is about . . . | My prediction was<br>CORRECT  INCORRECT |
| Excerpt 6 | I think today's excerpt is about . . . | My prediction was<br>CORRECT  INCORRECT |
| Excerpt 7 | I think today's excerpt is about . . . | My prediction was<br>CORRECT  INCORRECT |
| Excerpt 8 | I think today's excerpt is about . . . | My prediction was<br>CORRECT  INCORRECT |

| Part 3: After you read the book: | |
|---|---|
| Step 1: *Verify your initial prediction.* | My initial prediction was<br>CORRECT          INCORRECT |

**Lesson 1**

Book Title _____

# Question-Generation Chart

Name _____ Date _____

| Part 1: Generate literal questions. | Part 2: Generate inferential questions. |
|---|---|
| *Write one of the following questions and its answer.* | *Write one of the following questions and its answer.* |
| Who _____? What _____? | How do you think _____ felt when _____? |
| Where _____? When _____? | Why would _____ act the way he/she/they acted? |
| Why _____? How _____? | How would the story have changed if _____? |
| Other literal questions: _____ | Other inferential questions: _____ |
| **Excerpt 1** | |
| **Excerpt 2** | |
| **Excerpt 3** | |
| **Excerpt 4** | |
| **Excerpt 5** | |
| **Excerpt 6** | |
| **Excerpt 7** | |
| **Excerpt 8** | |

Book Title _____

# Clarification Chart

Name _____ Date _____

| Part 1: Reread and adjust reading rate. | |
|---|---|
| **Part 2: Decode multipart words.** | **Part 3: Use word-learning strategies.** |
| | Step 1: Use context clues. |
| | Step 2: Use a glossary. |
| | Step 3: Use a dictionary or an online dictionary. |
| Excerpt 1 | |
| Excerpt 2 | |
| Excerpt 3 | |
| Excerpt 4 | |
| Excerpt 5 | |
| Excerpt 6 | |
| Excerpt 7 | |
| Excerpt 8 | |

**Lesson 1**

Book Title _____

# Summarization Chart

Name _____ Date _____

| | Part 1: Retell what happened. | | |
|---|---|---|---|
| | *(First, next, then . . . , finally)* | | |
| | **Part 2: Develop a gist.** | | |
| | **Step 1:** Whom or what the excerpt was about. | **Step 2:** The most important thing about the whom or what. | **Step 3:** The main idea in twenty words or fewer. (Begin with *This excerpt is about . . . .*) |
| | Excerpt 1 | | |
| | Excerpt 2 | | |
| | Excerpt 3 | | |
| | Excerpt 4 | | |

Lesson
1

Book Title _____

# Summarization Chart, continued

Name _____ Date _____

|  | | |
|---|---|---|
| **Excerpt 5** | | |
| **Excerpt 6** | | |
| **Excerpt 7** | | |
| **Excerpt 8** | | |
| | What was the conflict/problem? | What was the climax/turning point? | What was the resolution/outcome? |

Book Title _____

# Character-Analysis Chart

Name _____ Date _____

Main Character: _____

| | **Character Details**<br>(How does the main character look, act, think, or feel because of events or other characters?) | **Personal Connections**<br>(How does the character relate to text, self, world?) |
|---|---|---|
| **Excerpt 1** | | |
| **Excerpt 2** | | |
| **Excerpt 3** | | |
| **Excerpt 4** | | |
| **Excerpt 5** | | |
| **Excerpt 6** | | |
| **Excerpt 7** | | |
| **Excerpt 8** | | |

## Lesson 2

# Fluency Practice: Mental Imagery

Name _____ Date _____

## Mind Control

Although we rely on computers to do complicated tasks, the human brain is currently the only "computer" that allows us to move and control our bodies. That may be changing, however. New technology is allowing scientists to create computer implants that work directly with our brains.

Right now this technology is helping some disabled people communicate and move. An implant is placed in the brain of a person who cannot speak or move. The implant is connected to a computer. When the person thinks about talking or moving, the computer receives the signals.

A person with the implant can control a cursor on a computer, type, and communicate using e-mail. With the aid of the implant, the person also has the ability to play video games, control a television, and move a robotic arm. Although these may seem like small tasks to some people, completing the tasks is a big step for people who have injuries or diseases that have robbed them of the ability to move.

The brain implant works by sensing the signals that move between brain cells. Normally these signals eventually travel through the spinal cord and cause the body to move. The connections are not complete in someone with paralysis. The brain implant creates a new connection between the brain cells and something else—a computer—that can respond.

Of course, improvements must still be made. The sensors must be made to be more sensitive and to last for a longer period of time. Scientists must also develop a way to make the system wireless so the implant can be smaller and portable. However, the possibilities are amazing. This technology could change the lives of many people with paralysis. Brain implants could empower these people in new, exciting, and helpful ways as the technology improves. Eventually scientists hope to create speech devices and complex robotic arms and legs that will enable patients to move and function as they were not able to move or function before.

**Directions: Illustrate what you thought about.**

## Lesson 3

# Fluency Practice: Standardized Test

Name _____ Date _____

# Mind Control

Although we rely on computers to do complicated tasks, the human brain is currently the only "computer" that allows us to move and control our bodies. That may be changing, however. New technology is allowing scientists to create computer implants that work directly with our brains.

Right now this technology is helping some disabled people communicate and move. An implant is placed in the brain of a person who cannot speak or move. The implant is connected to a computer. When the person thinks about talking or moving, the computer receives the signals.

A person with the implant can control a cursor on a computer, type, and communicate using e-mail. With the aid of the implant, the person also has the ability to play video games, control a television, and move a robotic arm. Although these may seem like small tasks to some people, completing the tasks is a big step for people who have injuries or diseases that have robbed them of the ability to move.

The brain implant works by sensing the signals that move between brain cells. Normally these signals eventually travel through the spinal cord and cause the body to move. The connections are not complete in someone with paralysis. The brain implant creates a new connection between the brain cells and something else—a computer—that can respond.

Of course, improvements must still be made. The sensors must be made to be more sensitive and to last for a longer period of time. Scientists must also develop a way to make the system wireless so the implant can be smaller and portable. However, the possibilities are amazing. This technology could change the lives of many people with paralysis. Brain implants could empower these people in new, exciting, and helpful ways as the technology improves. Eventually scientists hope to create speech devices and complex robotic arms and legs that will enable patients to move and function as they were not able to move or function before.

Score _____ /8 = _____ %

**Directions: Take turns reading the questions. Answer the questions together.**

Level 1: "Remember" Questions—each worth 1 point

**For Level 1 questions, fill in the space next to the correct answer in your own Workbook.**

1. New technology is now allowing scientists to
   ○ a. create computer implants that work directly with damaged spinal cords.
   ○ b. create computer implants that work directly with improving sight.
   ○ c. create computer implants that work directly with improving speech.
   ○ d. create computer implants that work directly with our brains.

# Lesson 3

## Fluency Practice: Standardized Test, continued

Name _____ Date _____

2. What happens when a person with the implant thinks about talking or moving?
   ○ a. A computer calls a nurse for help.
   ○ b. A computer prints the person's thought.
   ○ c. A computer receives the signals.
   ○ d. A computer types what the person is going to say or do.

3. How could the computer implant help someone communicate?
   ○ a. By helping them control a cursor on a computer, type, and use e-mail
   ○ b. By typing their needs onto a computer screen for them
   ○ c. By helping them dial the phone and have a conversation
   ○ d. By helping them translate body language into verbal language

4. What are some tasks a person can do with the help of the implant?
   ○ a. Clean and do other household tasks
   ○ b. Play video games, control a television, and move a robotic arm
   ○ c. Drive a car and move around independently
   ○ d. Steer a powered wheelchair, shop for groceries, and cook a meal

> **Level 2:** "Understand" Questions—worth 2 points (2 points for correct answer,
> 1 point for partially correct answer, 0 points for incorrect answer)

**For the Level 2 questions, write the answer in the spaces provided in your own Workbook.**

5. Explain how the brain implant works._____
   _____
   _____
   _____
   _____

6. Explain some improvements that still need to be made to the implant. _____
   _____
   _____
   _____
   _____
   _____

**Lesson 4**

# Fluency Practice: Information Learned

Name _____ Date _____

## Mind Control

Although we rely on computers to do complicated tasks, the human brain is currently the only "computer" that allows us to move and control our bodies. That may be changing, however. New technology is allowing scientists to create computer implants that work directly with our brains.

Right now this technology is helping some disabled people communicate and move. An implant is placed in the brain of a person who cannot speak or move. The implant is connected to a computer. When the person thinks about talking or moving, the computer receives the signals.

A person with the implant can control a cursor on a computer, type, and communicate using e-mail. With the aid of the implant, the person also has the ability to play video games, control a television, and move a robotic arm. Although these may seem like small tasks to some people, completing the tasks is a big step for people who have injuries or diseases that have robbed them of the ability to move.

The brain implant works by sensing the signals that move between brain cells. Normally these signals eventually travel through the spinal cord and cause the body to move. The connections are not complete in someone with paralysis. The brain implant creates a new connection between the brain cells and something else—a computer—that can respond.

Of course, improvements must still be made. The sensors must be made to be more sensitive and to last for a longer period of time. Scientists must also develop a way to make the system wireless so the implant can be smaller and portable. However, the possibilities are amazing. This technology could change the lives of many people with paralysis. Brain implants could empower these people in new, exciting, and helpful ways as the technology improves. Eventually scientists hope to create speech devices and complex robotic arms and legs that will enable patients to move and function as they were not able to move or function before.

- - - - - - - - - - - - - - - - - - - - - - - - - - - - - - - - - - - - - - - - - - - - - - - - -

**Directions: Write three things you learned after reading the fluency passage.**

**1.** I learned _____

_____.

**2.** I learned _____

_____.

**3.** I learned _____

_____.

**Lesson 5**

# Think-Pair-Share

Name _____ Date _____

● ● ● ● ● ● ● ● ● ● ● ● ● ● ● ● ● ● ● ● ● ● ● ● ● ● ● ● ● ● ● ● ● ● ● ● ● ● ●

### Analyze

Suppose you're a newspaper reporter asked to interview Phineas Gage. *Analyze* Gage's experiences, and generate two questions you could ask him. Provide answers to your questions as if Phineas Gage were talking.

Activity 1

Lesson 2

# Fluency Practice: Mental Imagery

Name ______________________________ Date ______________

## What Happened to Einstein's Brain?

Albert Einstein was arguably one of the most intelligent people to ever walk the Earth. His brilliant ideas opened up new areas of science that had never been imagined. After Einstein's death in 1955, some scientists wondered if the source of Einstein's genius could be found by examining his brain. The pathologist who performed Einstein's autopsy saved the brain and took many pictures of it. But then the brain disappeared.

Though the photographs of Einstein's brain were interesting to scientists, as brain science advanced, scientists wished for the actual brain to examine. Yet no one knew what had happened to the brain. Most people assumed the brain had been destroyed after the autopsy. In 1978, however, that claim was disproved when Einstein's brain was found by a reporter. The brain had been cut into several pieces, which were stored in glass jars in the office of the pathologist who had performed the autopsy. Strangely, the brain parts had been stored in two jars labeled as apple cider.

When scientists studied the brain, they learned several things. The section of Einstein's brain responsible for mathematical thought is larger than that section in most other human brains. Einstein's brain also contains more glial cells than the typical human brain. These cells are known as the "support" of the nervous system. It's important to note, however, that some scientists believe the glial study was not done properly, and they dispute the results of this study.

Another interesting thing about Einstein's brain is the fact that parts of the frontal lobe are missing. These areas, including a border between two areas called the lateral sulcus, are thought to contribute to language and communication. Some scientists think the lack of this brain tissue may have caused Einstein to think using mostly images instead of words. It is also possible that because some of this part of the brain was missing, his brain was able to transmit thoughts and images more quickly than most people's brains.

**Directions: Illustrate what you thought about.**

# Lesson 3

# Fluency Practice: Standardized Test

Name _____ Date _____

## What Happened to Einstein's Brain?

Albert Einstein was arguably one of the most intelligent people to ever walk the Earth. His brilliant ideas opened up new areas of science that had never been imagined. After Einstein's death in 1955, some scientists wondered if the source of Einstein's genius could be found by examining his brain. The pathologist who performed Einstein's autopsy saved the brain and took many pictures of it. But then the brain disappeared.

Though the photographs of Einstein's brain were interesting to scientists, as brain science advanced, scientists wished for the actual brain to examine. Yet no one knew what had happened to the brain. Most people assumed the brain had been destroyed after the autopsy. In 1978, however, that claim was disproved when Einstein's brain was found by a reporter. The brain had been cut into several pieces, which were stored in glass jars in the office of the pathologist who had performed the autopsy. Strangely, the brain parts had been stored in two jars labeled as apple cider.

When scientists studied the brain, they learned several things. The section of Einstein's brain responsible for mathematical thought is larger than that section in most other human brains. Einstein's brain also contains more glial cells than the typical human brain. These cells are known as the "support" of the nervous system. It's important to note, however, that some scientists believe the glial study was not done properly, and they dispute the results of this study.

Another interesting thing about Einstein's brain is the fact that parts of the frontal lobe are missing. These areas, including a border between two areas called the lateral sulcus, are thought to contribute to language and communication. Some scientists think the lack of this brain tissue may have caused Einstein to think using mostly images instead of words. It is also possible that because some of this part of the brain was missing, his brain was able to transmit thoughts and images more quickly than most people's brains.

Score _____ /8 = _____ %

**Directions: Take turns reading the questions. Answer the questions together.**

| Level 1: "Remember" Questions—each worth 1 point |

**For Level 1 questions, fill in the space next to the correct answer in your own Workbook.**

1. Which subject area did Einstein's ideas help advance?
   - ○ a. Reading
   - ○ b. Psychology
   - ○ c. Science
   - ○ d. Social studies

# Fluency Practice: Standardized Test, continued

Name _____ Date _____

2. Who performed Einstein's autopsy after he died?
   ○ a. A pathologist          ○ c. A surgeon
   ○ b. A nurse                ○ d. A pediatrician

3. When Einstein's brain disappeared after the autopsy, most people assumed
   ○ a. the brain was sent to a medical school.
   ○ b. the brain was buried with Einstein.
   ○ c. the brain was stolen.
   ○ d. the brain was destroyed.

4. Who found Einstein's brain in 1978?
   ○ a. A reporter            ○ c. A detective
   ○ b. A doctor              ○ d. A scientist

---

**Level 2:** "Understand" Questions—worth 2 points (2 points for correct answer, 1 point for partially correct answer, 0 points for incorrect answer)

---

**For the Level 2 questions, write the answer in the spaces provided in your own Workbook.**

5. Explain how Einstein's brain is different from most other human brains. _____

_____

_____

_____

_____

_____

6. Explain what was missing from Einstein's brain and how this may have affected the way he thought. _____

_____

_____

_____

_____

_____

**Lesson 4**

Book Title _____

# Story-Components Chart

Name _____ Date _____

| |
|---|
| **Author(s):** |
| **Illustrator(s)** (if any): |
| **Genre:**<br><br>☐ Fiction  ☐ Nonfiction |
| **Theme:**<br>What is the moral of the story? |
| **Perspective:**<br>What is the point of view of the story?<br><br>☐ First person  ☐ Second person  ☐ Third person |
| **Mood:**<br>How did you feel while you read the story? |
| **Author's Purpose:**<br>Why did the author(s) write the story?<br><br>☐ To persuade  ☐ To inform  ☐ To entertain |

## Lesson 4

# Fluency Practice: Information Learned

Name _____ Date _____

## What Happened to Einstein's Brain?

Albert Einstein was arguably one of the most intelligent people to ever walk the Earth. His brilliant ideas opened up new areas of science that had never been imagined. After Einstein's death in 1955, some scientists wondered if the source of Einstein's genius could be found by examining his brain. The pathologist who performed Einstein's autopsy saved the brain and took many pictures of it. But then the brain disappeared.

Though the photographs of Einstein's brain were interesting to scientists, as brain science advanced, scientists wished for the actual brain to examine. Yet no one knew what had happened to the brain. Most people assumed the brain had been destroyed after the autopsy. In 1978, however, that claim was disproved when Einstein's brain was found by a reporter. The brain had been cut into several pieces, which were stored in glass jars in the office of the pathologist who had performed the autopsy. Strangely, the brain parts had been stored in two jars labeled as apple cider.

When scientists studied the brain, they learned several things. The section of Einstein's brain responsible for mathematical thought is larger than that section in most other human brains. Einstein's brain also contains more glial cells than the typical human brain. These cells are known as the "support" of the nervous system. It's important to note, however, that some scientists believe the glial study was not done properly, and they dispute the results of this study.

Another interesting thing about Einstein's brain is the fact that parts of the frontal lobe are missing. These areas, including a border between two areas called the lateral sulcus, are thought to contribute to language and communication. Some scientists think the lack of this brain tissue may have caused Einstein to think using mostly images instead of words. It is also possible that because some of this part of the brain was missing, his brain was able to transmit thoughts and images more quickly than most people's brains.

. . . . . . . . . . . . . . . . . . . . . . . . . . . . . . . . . . . . . . . . . .

**Directions: Write three things you learned after reading the fluency passage.**

**1.** I learned _____

_____.

**2.** I learned _____

_____.

**3.** I learned _____

**Lesson 5**

# Think-Pair-Share

Name _____ Date _____

**Use the Think-Pair-Share Strategy to complete the question below.**

Step 1: **Think** about the question for one minute.

Step 2: **Pair,** and complete the question with your partner.

Step 3: **Share** what you wrote with the class.

• • • • • • • • • • • • • • • • • • • • • • • • • • • • • • • • • • • • • • • • • • •

**Evaluate**

*Evaluate* the life and experiences of Phineas Gage, and compare these experiences to any other main characters you've read about in this program. Which main character do you think showed the most strength and courage in the face of challenges? Give three reasons you feel this way.

**Lesson**
**1**

Book Title _____

# Reciprocal-Teaching Chart

Name _____ Date _____

**Group Members:**

Discussion Leader/Passage Selector _____    Predictor/Character Analyzer _____

Question Generator _____    Clarifier _____    Summarizer _____

| **Prediction of Excerpt** | **Character Analysis** |
|---|---|
| _____ | Character details: _____ |
| _____ | _____ |
| _____ | _____ |
| _____ | Personal connections: _____ |
| **Verification** | _____ |
| CORRECT    INCORRECT | _____ |
| | _____ |
| **Question Generation** | **Clarification** |
| Literal question: _____ | Word 1: _____ |
| _____ | Definition: _____ |
| Answer: _____ | _____ |
| _____ | _____ |
| Inferential question: _____ | Word 2: _____ |
| _____ | Definition: _____ |
| Answer: _____ | _____ |
| **Summarization** | **Passage Selected** |
| Whom or what: _____ | Page number: _____ |
| Most important thing: _____ | Comments about passage: _____ |
| _____ | _____ |
| Main idea: | _____ |
| ____ ____ ____ ____ ____ | _____ |
| ____ ____ ____ ____ ____ | _____ |
| ____ ____ ____ ____ ____ | _____ |
| ____ ____ ____ ____ ____ | _____ |

Lesson
**2**

Book Title _____

# Reciprocal-Teaching Chart

Name _____ Date _____

**Group
Members:**

Discussion Leader/Passage Selector _____ Predictor/Character Analyzer _____

Question Generator _____ Clarifier _____ Summarizer _____

| **Prediction of Excerpt** | **Character Analysis** |
|---|---|
| _____ | Character details: _____ |
| _____ | _____ |
| _____ | Personal connections: _____ |
| **Verification** | _____ |
| | _____ |
| CORRECT    INCORRECT | _____ |
| **Question Generation** | **Clarification** |
| Literal question: _____ | Word 1: _____ |
| _____ | Definition: _____ |
| Answer: _____ | _____ |
| _____ | |
| Inferential question: _____ | Word 2: _____ |
| _____ | Definition: _____ |
| Answer: _____ | _____ |
| **Summarization** | **Passage Selected** |
| Whom or what: _____ | Page number: _____ |
| Most important thing: _____ | Comments about passage: _____ |
| | _____ |
| Main idea: | _____ |
| _____ _____ _____ | _____ |
| _____ _____ _____ | _____ |
| _____ _____ _____ | _____ |
| _____ _____ _____ | _____ |

# Fluency Practice: Mental Imagery

Name _____ Date _____

## Hatchet

Brian Robeson stared out the window of the small plane at the endless green northern wilderness below. It was a small plane, a Cessna 406—a bushplane—and the engine was so loud, so roaring and consuming and loud, that it ruined any chance for conversation.

Not that he had much to say. He was thirteen and the only passenger on the plane was a pilot named—what was it? Jim or Jake or something—who was in his mid-forties and who had been silent as he worked to prepare for takeoff. In fact since Brian had come to the small airport in Hampton, New York to meet the plane—driven by his mother—the pilot had only spoken five words to him.

"Get in the copilot's seat."

Which Brian had done. They had taken off and that was the last of the conversation. There had been the initial excitement, of course. He had never flown in a single-engine plane before and to be sitting in the copilot's seat with all the controls right there in front of him, all the instruments in his face as the plane clawed for altitude, jerking and sliding on the wind currents as the pilot took off, had been interesting and exciting. But in five minutes they had leveled off at six thousand feet and headed northwest and from then on the pilot had been silent, staring out the front, and the drone of the engine had been all that was left. The drone and the sea of green trees that lay before the plane's nose and flowed to the horizon, spread with lakes, swamps, and wandering streams and rivers.

Now Brian sat, looking out the window with the roar thundering through his ears, and tried to catalog what had led up to his taking this flight.

The thinking started.

Always it started with a single word.

Divorce.

It was an ugly word, he thought. A tearing, ugly word that meant fights and yelling, lawyers—God, he thought, how he hated lawyers who sat with their comfortable smiles and tried to explain to him in legal terms how all that he lived in was coming apart—and the breaking and shattering of all the solid things.

**Directions: Illustrate what you thought about.**

**Lesson 3**

Book Title _____

# Reciprocal-Teaching Chart

Name _____  Date _____

**Group Members:**

Discussion Leader/Passage Selector _____  Predictor/Character Analyzer _____

Question Generator _____  Clarifier _____  Summarizer _____

| **Prediction of Excerpt** | **Character Analysis** |
|---|---|
| _____ | Character details: _____ |
| _____ | _____ |
| _____ | _____ |
| _____ | Personal connections: _____ |
| **Verification** | _____ |
| | _____ |
| CORRECT    INCORRECT | _____ |
| | _____ |

| **Question Generation** | **Clarification** |
|---|---|
| Literal question: _____ | Word 1: _____ |
| _____ | Definition: _____ |
| Answer: _____ | _____ |
| | _____ |
| Inferential question: _____ | Word 2: _____ |
| _____ | Definition: _____ |
| Answer: _____ | _____ |

| **Summarization** | **Passage Selected** |
|---|---|
| Whom or what: _____ | Page number: _____ |
| Most important thing: _____ | Comments about passage: _____ |
| _____ | _____ |
| Main idea: | _____ |
| ____ ____ ____ ____ ____ | _____ |
| ____ ____ ____ ____ ____ | _____ |
| ____ ____ ____ ____ ____ | _____ |
| ____ ____ ____ ____ ____ . | _____ |

**Lesson 3**

# Fluency Practice: Standardized Test

Name _____ Date _____

## Hatchet

Brian Robeson stared out the window of the small plane at the endless green northern wilderness below. It was a small plane, a Cessna 406—a bushplane—and the engine was so loud, so roaring and consuming and loud, that it ruined any chance for conversation.

Not that he had much to say. He was thirteen and the only passenger on the plane was a pilot named—what was it? Jim or Jake or something—who was in his mid-forties and who had been silent as he worked to prepare for takeoff. In fact since Brian had come to the small airport in Hampton, New York to meet the plane—driven by his mother—the pilot had only spoken five words to him.

"Get in the copilot's seat."

Which Brian had done. They had taken off and that was the last of the conversation. There had been the initial excitement, of course. He had never flown in a single-engine plane before and to be sitting in the copilot's seat with all the controls right there in front of him, all the instruments in his face as the plane clawed for altitude, jerking and sliding

on the wind currents as the pilot took off, had been interesting and exciting. But in five minutes they had leveled off at six thousand feet and headed northwest and from then on the pilot had been silent, staring out the front, and the drone of the engine had been all that was left. The drone and the sea of green trees that lay before the plane's nose and flowed to the horizon, spread with lakes, swamps, and wandering streams and rivers.

Now Brian sat, looking out the window with the roar thundering through his ears, and tried to catalog what had led up to his taking this flight.

The thinking started.

Always it started with a single word.

Divorce.

It was an ugly word, he thought. A tearing, ugly word that meant fights and yelling, lawyers—God, he thought, how he hated lawyers who sat with their comfortable smiles and tried to explain to him in legal terms how all that he lived in was coming apart—and the breaking and shattering of all the solid things.

Score _____ /8 = _____ %

**Directions: Take turns reading the questions. Answer the questions together.**

**Level 1:** "Remember" Questions—each worth 1 point

**For Level 1 questions, fill in the space next to the correct answer in your own Workbook.**

1. Brian Robeson was flying in which type of plane?
   - ○ a. Casa 212
   - ○ b. Cessna 406
   - ○ c. Jetstream 41
   - ○ d. Boeing 747

## Lesson 3

# Fluency Practice: Standardized Test, continued

Name _____ Date _____

2. How old was Brian at the time of the flight?
   - ○ a. Sixteen years old       ○ c. Thirteen years old
   - ○ b. Eleven years old        ○ d. Fifteen years old

3. Where did Brian need to go to meet the plane?
   - ○ a. Hampton, New York
   - ○ b. Manchester, New Hampshire
   - ○ c. Hudson, Massachusetts
   - ○ d. Albany, New York

4. Where did Brian sit during the flight?
   - ○ a. In a seat facing backward.
   - ○ b. In first-class.
   - ○ c. In the back of the plane.
   - ○ d. In the copilot's seat.

---

**Level 2:** "Understand" Questions—worth 2 points (2 points for correct answer, 1 point for partially correct answer, 0 points for incorrect answer)

---

**For the Level 2 questions, write the answer in the spaces provided in your own Workbook.**

5. Explain how Brian was feeling as the plane was taking off and climbing to six thousand feet.

_____

_____

_____

_____

_____

6. Explain what was happening in Brian's life that led him to take the flight. _____

_____

_____

_____

_____

_____

## Lesson 4

Book Title _____

# Reciprocal-Teaching Chart

Name _____ Date _____

**Group Members:**

Discussion Leader/Passage Selector _____    Predictor/Character Analyzer _____

Question Generator _____    Clarifier _____    Summarizer _____

### Prediction of Excerpt

_____

_____

_____

_____

### Verification

CORRECT    INCORRECT

### Character Analysis

Character details: _____

_____

Personal connections: _____

_____

_____

_____

_____

### Question Generation

Literal question: _____

_____

Answer: _____

_____

Inferential question: _____

_____

Answer: _____

### Clarification

Word 1: _____

Definition: _____

_____

_____

Word 2: _____

Definition: _____

_____

### Summarization

Whom or what: _____

Most important thing: _____

Main idea:

_____  _____

_____

_____

_____

### Passage Selected

Page number: _____

Comments about passage: _____

_____

_____

_____

_____

_____

_____

**Lesson 4**

# Fluency Practice: Information Learned

Name _____ Date _____

## Hatchet

Brian Robeson stared out the window of the small plane at the endless green northern wilderness below. It was a small plane, a Cessna 406—a bushplane—and the engine was so loud, so roaring and consuming and loud, that it ruined any chance for conversation.

Not that he had much to say. He was thirteen and the only passenger on the plane was a pilot named—what was it? Jim or Jake or something—who was in his mid-forties and who had been silent as he worked to prepare for takeoff. In fact since Brian had come to the small airport in Hampton, New York to meet the plane—driven by his mother—the pilot had only spoken five words to him.

"Get in the copilot's seat."

Which Brian had done. They had taken off and that was the last of the conversation. There had been the initial excitement, of course. He had never flown in a single-engine plane before and to be sitting in the copilot's seat with all the controls right there in front of him, all the instruments in his face as the plane clawed for altitude, jerking and sliding on the wind currents as the pilot took off, had been interesting and exciting. But in five minutes they had leveled off at six thousand feet and headed northwest and from then on the pilot had been silent, staring out the front, and the drone of the engine had been all that was left. The drone and the sea of green trees that lay before the plane's nose and flowed to the horizon, spread with lakes, swamps, and wandering streams and rivers.

Now Brian sat, looking out the window with the roar thundering through his ears, and tried to catalog what had led up to his taking this flight.

The thinking started.

Always it started with a single word.

Divorce.

It was an ugly word, he thought. A tearing, ugly word that meant fights and yelling, lawyers—God, he thought, how he hated lawyers who sat with their comfortable smiles and tried to explain to him in legal terms how all that he lived in was coming apart—and the breaking and shattering of all the solid things.

**Directions:** Write three things you learned after reading the fluency passage.

1. I learned _____

_____.

2. I learned _____

_____.

3. I learned _____

_____.

## Lesson 5

# Think-Pair-Share

Name _____ Date _____

### Directions

**Use the Think-Pair-Share Strategy to complete the question below.**

Step 1: **Think** about the question for one minute.

Step 2: **Pair,** and complete the question with your partner.

Step 3: **Share** what you wrote with the class.

### Evaluate

*Evaluate* how Brian has handled the emergency on the plane. Would you have tried the same things he tried to save yourself? Why or why not?

**Lesson**

**1**

Book Title _____

# Reciprocal-Teaching Chart

Name _____ Date _____

**Group Members:**

Discussion Leader/Passage Selector _____ Predictor/Character Analyzer _____

Question Generator _____ Clarifier _____ Summarizer _____

| **Prediction of Excerpt** | **Character Analysis** |
|---|---|
| _____ | Character details: _____ |
| _____ | _____ |
| _____ | Personal connections: _____ |
| _____ | _____ |
| **Verification** | _____ |
| CORRECT    INCORRECT | _____ |

| **Question Generation** | **Clarification** |
|---|---|
| Literal question: _____ | Word 1: _____ |
| _____ | Definition: _____ |
| Answer: _____ | _____ |
| _____ | _____ |
| Inferential question: _____ | Word 2: _____ |
| _____ | Definition: _____ |
| Answer: _____ | _____ |

| **Summarization** | **Passage Selected** |
|---|---|
| Whom or what: _____ | Page number: _____ |
| Most important thing: _____ | Comments about passage: _____ |
| _____ | _____ |
| Main idea: | _____ |
| _____ | _____ |
| _____ | _____ |
| _____ | _____ |
| _____ | _____ |

## Lesson 2

Book Title _____

# Reciprocal-Teaching Chart

Name _____ Date _____

**Group Members:**

Discussion Leader/Passage Selector _____  Predictor/Character Analyzer _____

Question Generator _____  Clarifier _____  Summarizer _____

| **Prediction of Excerpt** | **Character Analysis** |
|---|---|
| _____ | Character details: _____ |
| _____ | _____ |
| _____ | _____ |
| _____ | Personal connections: _____ |
| **Verification** | _____ |
| | _____ |
| CORRECT    INCORRECT | _____ |
| **Question Generation** | **Clarification** |
| Literal question: _____ | Word 1: _____ |
| _____ | Definition: _____ |
| Answer: _____ | _____ |
| | _____ |
| Inferential question: _____ | Word 2: _____ |
| _____ | Definition: _____ |
| Answer: _____ | _____ |
| **Summarization** | **Passage Selected** |
| Whom or what: _____ | Page number: _____ |
| Most important thing: _____ | Comments about passage: _____ |
| _____ | _____ |
| Main idea: | _____ |
| _____ | _____ |
| _____ | _____ |
| _____ | _____ |
| _____ | _____ |

## Lesson 2

# Fluency Practice: Mental Imagery

Name _____ Date _____

## Hatchet

Going to die, Brian thought. Going to die, gonna die, gonna die—his whole brain screamed it in the sudden silence.

Gonna die.

He wiped his mouth with the back of his arm and held the nose down. The plane went into a glide, a very fast glide that ate altitude, and suddenly there weren't any lakes. All he'd seen since they started flying over the forest was lakes and now they were gone. Gone. Out in front, far away at the horizon, he could see lots of them, glittering blue in the late afternoon sun.

But he needed one right in front. He desperately needed a lake right in front of the plane and all he saw through the windshield were trees, green death trees. If he had to turn—if he had to turn he didn't think he could keep the plane flying. His stomach tightened into a series of rolling knots and his breath came in short bursts . . .

There!

Not quite in front but slightly to the right he saw a lake. L-shaped, with rounded corners, and the plane was nearly aimed at the long part of the L, coming from the bottom and heading to the top. Just a tiny bit to the right. He pushed the right rudder pedal gently and the nose moved over.

But the turn cost him speed and now the lake was above the nose. He pulled back on the wheel slightly and the nose came up. This caused the plane to slow dramatically and almost seem to stop and wallow in the air. The controls became very loose-feeling and frightened Brian, making him push the wheel back in. This increased the speed a bit but filled the windshield once more with nothing but trees, and put the lake well above the nose and out of reach.

For a space of three or four seconds things seemed to hang, almost to stop. The plane was flying, but so slowly, so slowly . . . it would never reach the lake. Brian looked out to the side and saw a small pond and at the edge of the pond some large animal—he thought a moose—standing out in the water. All so still looking, so stopped, the pond and the moose and the trees, as he slid over them now only three or four hundred feet off the ground—all like a picture.

• • • • • • • • • • • • • • • • • • • • • • • • • • • • • • • • • • • • • •

**Directions: Illustrate what you thought about.**

## Lesson 3

Book Title _____

# Reciprocal-Teaching Chart

Name _____ Date _____

**Group Members:**

Discussion Leader/Passage Selector _____ Predictor/Character Analyzer _____

Question Generator _____ Clarifier _____ Summarizer _____

| **Prediction of Excerpt** | **Character Analysis** |
|---|---|
| _____ | Character details: _____ |
| _____ | _____ |
| _____ | Personal connections: _____ |
| **Verification** | _____ |
| CORRECT     INCORRECT | _____ |
| **Question Generation** | **Clarification** |
| Literal question: _____ | Word 1: _____ |
| _____ | Definition: _____ |
| Answer: _____ | _____ |
| _____ | _____ |
| Inferential question: _____ | Word 2: _____ |
| | Definition: _____ |
| Answer: _____ | _____ |
| **Summarization** | **Passage Selected** |
| Whom or what: _____ | Page number: _____ |
| Most important thing: _____ | Comments about passage: _____ |
| Main idea: | _____ |
| _____ | _____ |
| _____ | _____ |
| _____ | _____ |
| _____ | _____ |

**Lesson 3**

# Fluency Practice: Standardized Test

Name _____ Date _____

## Hatchet

Going to die, Brian thought. Going to die, gonna die, gonna die—his whole brain screamed it in the sudden silence.

Gonna die.

He wiped his mouth with the back of his arm and held the nose down. The plane went into a glide, a very fast glide that ate altitude, and suddenly there weren't any lakes. All he'd seen since they started flying over the forest was lakes and now they were gone. Gone. Out in front, far away at the horizon, he could see lots of them, glittering blue in the late afternoon sun.

But he needed one right in front. He desperately needed a lake right in front of the plane and all he saw through the windshield were trees, green death trees. If he had to turn— if he had to turn he didn't think he could keep the plane flying. His stomach tightened into a series of rolling knots and his breath came in short bursts . . .

There!

Not quite in front but slightly to the right he saw a lake. L-shaped, with rounded corners, and the plane was nearly aimed at the long part of the L, coming from the bottom and heading to the top. Just a tiny bit to the right. He pushed the right rudder pedal gently and the nose moved over.

But the turn cost him speed and now the lake was above the nose. He pulled back on the wheel slightly and the nose came up. This caused the plane to slow dramatically and almost seem to stop and wallow in the air. The controls became very loose-feeling and frightened Brian, making him push the wheel back in. This increased the speed a bit but filled the windshield once more with nothing but trees, and put the lake well above the nose and out of reach.

For a space of three or four seconds things seemed to hang, almost to stop. The plane was flying, but so slowly, so slowly . . . it would never reach the lake. Brian looked out to the side and saw a small pond and at the edge of the pond some large animal—he thought a moose— standing out in the water. All so still looking, so stopped, the pond and the moose and the trees, as he slid over them now only three or four hundred feet off the ground—all like a picture.

Score _____ /8 = _____ %

**Directions: Take turns reading the questions. Answer the questions together.**

**Level 1:** "Remember" Questions—each worth 1 point

**For Level 1 questions, fill in the space next to the correct answer in your own Workbook.**

**1.** As the plane was going down, Brian desperately needed a lake in front of him. What did he see instead?

○ a. Sand
○ b. Snow
○ c. Trees
○ d. Mountains

**Lesson**

**3**

# Fluency Practice: Standardized Test, continued

Name _____ Date _____

**2.** What did Brian think would happen if he had to turn the plane?

   ◯ a. He would send the plane into a steep nosedive.

   ◯ b. He would be able to fly the plane back in line with the horizon.

   ◯ c. He would roll the plane over and over in the sky.

   ◯ d. He wouldn't be able to keep the plane flying.

**3.** Where did Brian want to land the plane?

   ◯ a. In a lake.          ◯ c. In a pasture.

   ◯ b. In a sand dune.      ◯ d. In a stretch of land near a creek.

**4.** What happened to the plane when Brian pulled back on the wheel?

   ◯ a. It increased speed.

   ◯ b. The nose came up.

   ◯ c. The landing gear came out.

   ◯ d. It dropped all its fuel.

---

**Level 2:** "Understand" Questions—worth 2 points (2 points for correct answer, 1 point for partially correct answer, 0 points for incorrect answer)

---

**For the Level 2 questions, write the answer in the spaces provided in your own Workbook.**

**5.** Explain what happened that made the lake out of reach for Brian's landing.

_____

_____

_____

_____

_____

**6.** Explain what Brian saw as he flew only three or four hundred feet off the ground.

_____

_____

_____

_____

_____

Lesson
4

Book Title _____

# Reciprocal-Teaching Chart

Name _____ Date _____

**Group Members:**

Discussion Leader/Passage Selector _____    Predictor/Character Analyzer _____

Question Generator _____    Clarifier _____    Summarizer _____

| **Prediction of Excerpt** | **Character Analysis** |
|---|---|
| _____ | Character details: _____ |
| _____ | _____ |
| _____ | _____ |
| _____ | Personal connections: _____ |
| **Verification** | _____ |
| | _____ |
| CORRECT    INCORRECT | _____ |
| **Question Generation** | **Clarification** |
| Literal question: _____ | Word 1: _____ |
| _____ | Definition: _____ |
| Answer: _____ | _____ |
| _____ | _____ |
| Inferential question: _____ | Word 2: _____ |
| _____ | Definition: _____ |
| Answer: _____ | _____ |
| **Summarization** | **Passage Selected** |
| Whom or what: _____ | Page number: _____ |
| Most important thing: _____ | Comments about passage: _____ |
| _____ | _____ |
| Main idea: | _____ |
| _____ | _____ |
| _____ | _____ |
| _____ | _____ |
| _____ | _____ |

**Lesson 4**

# Fluency Practice: Information Learned

Name _____ Date _____

## Hatchet

Going to die, Brian thought. Going to die, gonna die, gonna die—his whole brain screamed it in the sudden silence.

Gonna die.

He wiped his mouth with the back of his arm and held the nose down. The plane went into a glide, a very fast glide that ate altitude, and suddenly there weren't any lakes. All he'd seen since they started flying over the forest was lakes and now they were gone. Gone. Out in front, far away at the horizon, he could see lots of them, glittering blue in the late afternoon sun.

But he needed one right in front. He desperately needed a lake right in front of the plane and all he saw through the windshield were trees, green death trees. If he had to turn— if he had to turn he didn't think he could keep the plane flying. His stomach tightened into a series of rolling knots and his breath came in short bursts . . .

There!

Not quite in front but slightly to the right he saw a lake. L-shaped, with rounded corners, and the plane was nearly aimed at the long part of the L, coming from the bottom and heading to the top. Just a tiny bit to the right. He pushed the right rudder pedal gently and the nose moved over.

But the turn cost him speed and now the lake was above the nose. He pulled back on the wheel slightly and the nose came up. This caused the plane to slow dramatically and almost seem to stop and wallow in the air. The controls became very loose-feeling and frightened Brian, making him push the wheel back in. This increased the speed a bit but filled the windshield once more with nothing but trees, and put the lake well above the nose and out of reach.

For a space of three or four seconds things seemed to hang, almost to stop. The plane was flying, but so slowly, so slowly . . . it would never reach the lake. Brian looked out to the side and saw a small pond and at the edge of the pond some large animal—he thought a moose— standing out in the water. All so still looking, so stopped, the pond and the moose and the trees, as he slid over them now only three or four hundred feet off the ground—all like a picture.

• • • • • • • • • • • • • • • • • • • • • • • • • • • • • • • • • • • • • • • • • •

**Directions: Write three things you learned after reading the fluency passage.**

**1.** I learned _____

_____.

**2.** I learned _____

_____.

**3.** I learned _____

_____.

## Think-Pair-Share

Name _____ Date _____

Use the Think-Pair-Share Strategy to complete the question below.

Step 1: **Think** about the question for one minute.

Step 2: **Pair,** and complete the question with your partner.

Step 3: **Share** what you wrote with the class.

**Evaluate**

*Evaluate* Brian's situation, and put together a survival kit with four items you think he needs the most. Provide an explanation for each item you choose.

Lesson 1

# Reciprocal-Teaching Chart

Name _____ Date _____

**Group Members:**

_____ | _____
Discussion Leader/Passage Selector | Predictor/Character Analyzer

_____ | _____ | _____
Question Generator | Clarifier | Summarizer

### Prediction of Excerpt

_____

_____

_____

_____

### Verification

CORRECT      INCORRECT

### Question Generation

Literal question: _____

_____

Answer: _____

_____

Inferential question: _____

_____

Answer: _____

### Summarization

Whom or what: _____

Most important thing: _____

_____

Main idea:

_____  _____  _____

_____  _____  _____

_____  _____  _____

_____

_____  _____  _____ .

### Character Analysis

Character details: _____

_____

_____

Personal connections: _____

_____

_____

_____

### Clarification

Word 1: _____

Definition: _____

_____

_____

Word 2: _____

Definition: _____

_____

### Passage Selected

Page number: _____

Comments about passage: _____

_____

_____

_____

_____

_____

_____

Lesson
**2**

Book Title _____

# Reciprocal-Teaching Chart

Name _____ Date _____

**Group Members:**

Discussion Leader/Passage Selector _____ Predictor/Character Analyzer _____

Question Generator _____ Clarifier _____ Summarizer _____

| **Prediction of Excerpt** | **Character Analysis** |
|---|---|
| _____ | Character details: _____ |
| _____ | _____ |
| _____ | _____ |
| _____ | Personal connections: _____ |
| **Verification** | _____ |
| | _____ |
| CORRECT     INCORRECT | _____ |

| **Question Generation** | **Clarification** |
|---|---|
| Literal question: _____ | Word 1: _____ |
| _____ | Definition: _____ |
| Answer: _____ | _____ |
| _____ | _____ |
| Inferential question: _____ | Word 2: _____ |
| _____ | Definition: _____ |
| Answer: _____ | _____ |

| **Summarization** | **Passage Selected** |
|---|---|
| Whom or what: _____ | Page number: _____ |
| Most important thing: _____ | Comments about passage: _____ |
| | _____ |
| Main idea: | _____ |
| _____  _____  _____ | _____ |
| _____  _____  _____ | _____ |
| _____  _____  _____ | _____ |
| _____  _____  _____ | _____ |

# Fluency Practice: Mental Imagery

Name _____ Date _____

## Hatchet

It was still very early, only just past true dawn, and the water was so calm he could see his reflection. It frightened him—the face was cut and bleeding—swollen and lumpy, the hair all matted, and on his forehead a cut had healed but left the hair stuck with blood and scab. His eyes were slits in the bites and he was—somehow—covered with dirt. He slapped the water with his hand to destroy the mirror.

Ugly, he thought. Very, very ugly.

And he was, at that moment, almost overcome with self-pity. He was dirty and starving and bitten and hurt and lonely and ugly and afraid and so completely miserable that it was like being in a pit, a dark, deep pit with no way out.

He sat back on the bank and fought crying. Then let it come and cried for perhaps three, four minutes. Long tears, self-pity tears, wasted tears.

He stood, went back to the water, and took small drinks. As soon as the cold water hit his stomach he felt the hunger sharpen, as it had before, and he stood and held his abdomen until the hunger cramps receded.

He had to eat. He was weak with it again, down with the hunger, and he had to eat.

Back at the shelter the berries lay in a pile where he had dumped them when he grabbed his windbreaker—gut cherries he called them in his mind now—and he thought of eating some of them. Not such a crazy amount, as he had, which he felt brought on the sickness in the night—but just enough to stave off the hunger a bit.

He crawled into the shelter. Some flies were on the berries and he brushed them off. He selected only the berries that were solidly ripe—not the light red ones, but the berries that were dark, maroon red to black and swollen in ripeness. When he had a small handful of them he went back down to the lake and washed them in the water—small fish scattered away when he splashed the water up and he wished he had a fishing line and hook—then he ate them carefully, spitting out the pits. They were still tart, but had a sweetness to them, although they seemed to make his lips a bit numb.

When he finished he was still hungry, but the edge was gone and his legs didn't feel as weak as they had.

**Directions: Illustrate what you thought about.**

Book Title _____

## Reciprocal-Teaching Chart

**Lesson 3**

Name _____ Date _____

**Group Members:**

Discussion Leader/Passage Selector _____    Predictor/Character Analyzer _____

Question Generator _____    Clarifier _____    Summarizer _____

| **Prediction of Excerpt** | **Character Analysis** |
|---|---|
| _____ | Character details: _____ |
| _____ | _____ |
| _____ | _____ |
| _____ | Personal connections: _____ |
| **Verification** | _____ |
| CORRECT    INCORRECT | _____ |

| **Question Generation** | **Clarification** |
|---|---|
| Literal question: _____ | Word 1: _____ |
| _____ | Definition: _____ |
| Answer: _____ | _____ |
| _____ | _____ |
| Inferential question: _____ | Word 2: _____ |
| _____ | Definition: _____ |
| Answer: _____ | _____ |

| **Summarization** | **Passage Selected** |
|---|---|
| Whom or what: _____ | Page number: _____ |
| Most important thing: _____ | Comments about passage: _____ |
| Main idea: | _____ |
| ___ ___ ___ ___ | _____ |
| ___ ___ ___ ___ | _____ |
| ___ ___ ___ ___ | _____ |

## Lesson 3

# Fluency Practice: Standardized Test

Name _____ Date _____

## Hatchet

It was still very early, only just past true dawn, and the water was so calm he could see his reflection. It frightened him—the face was cut and bleeding—swollen and lumpy, the hair all matted, and on his forehead a cut had healed but left the hair stuck with blood and scab. His eyes were slits in the bites and he was—somehow—covered with dirt. He slapped the water with his hand to destroy the mirror.

Ugly, he thought. Very, very ugly.

And he was, at that moment, almost overcome with self-pity. He was dirty and starving and bitten and hurt and lonely and ugly and afraid and so completely miserable that it was like being in a pit, a dark, deep pit with no way out.

He sat back on the bank and fought crying. Then let it come and cried for perhaps three, four minutes. Long tears, self-pity tears, wasted tears.

He stood, went back to the water, and took small drinks. As soon as the cold water hit his stomach he felt the hunger sharpen, as it had before, and he stood and held his abdomen until the hunger cramps receded.

He had to eat. He was weak with it again, down with the hunger, and he had to eat.

Back at the shelter the berries lay in a pile where he had dumped them when he grabbed his windbreaker—gut cherries he called them in his mind now—and he thought of eating some of them. Not such a crazy amount, as he had, which he felt brought on the sickness in the night—but just enough to stave off the hunger a bit.

He crawled into the shelter. Some flies were on the berries and he brushed them off. He selected only the berries that were solidly ripe—not the light red ones, but the berries that were dark, maroon red to black and swollen in ripeness. When he had a small handful of them he went back down to the lake and washed them in the water—small fish scattered away when he splashed the water up and he wished he had a fishing line and hook—then he ate them carefully, spitting out the pits. They were still tart, but had a sweetness to them, although they seemed to make his lips a bit numb.

When he finished he was still hungry, but the edge was gone and his legs didn't feel as weak as they had.

**Score** _____ /8 = _____ %

**Directions: Take turns reading the questions. Answer the questions together.**

| Level 1: "Remember" Questions—each worth 1 point |
| --- |

**For Level 1 questions, fill in the space next to the correct answer in your own Workbook.**

1. What time of day was Brian looking at his reflection in the water?
   - ○ a. Just past dusk
   - ○ b. Late afternoon
   - ○ c. Midmorning
   - ○ d. Just past dawn

# Fluency Practice: Standardized Test, continued

Name _____ Date _____

**2.** Why did Brian slap the water with his hand?
- ○ a. He thought his reflection looked very ugly.
- ○ b. He missed his parents.
- ○ c. He was trying to scare away hungry animals.
- ○ d. He thought the slap would attract fish to catch.

**3.** As Brian sat on the bank, which emotion almost overcame him?
- ○ a. Anger
- ○ b. Optimism
- ○ c. Self-pity
- ○ d. Nervousness

**4.** What happened after the cold water hit Brian's stomach?
- ○ a. He felt his hunger get worse.
- ○ b. He felt as though he was going to get sick.
- ○ c. He felt very tired.
- ○ d. He felt his lips go numb.

> **Level 2:** "Understand" Questions—worth 2 points (2 points for correct answer, 1 point for partially correct answer, 0 points for incorrect answer)

**For the Level 2 questions, write the answer in the spaces provided in your own Workbook.**

**5.** Explain what Brian was going to do to be less hungry. _____

_____

_____

_____

_____

**6.** Explain what Brian actually did with the cherries he had in the shelter. _____

_____

_____

_____

_____

Lesson
4

Book Title _____

# Reciprocal-Teaching Chart

Name _____ Date _____

**Group Members:**

_____        _____
Discussion Leader/Passage Selector        Predictor/Character Analyzer

_____        _____
Question Generator          Clarifier          Summarizer

| **Prediction of Excerpt** | **Character Analysis** |
|---|---|

**Prediction of Excerpt**

_____

_____

_____

**Verification**

CORRECT          INCORRECT

**Character Analysis**

Character details: _____

_____

_____

Personal connections: _____

_____

_____

_____

**Question Generation**

Literal question: _____

_____

Answer: _____

_____

Inferential question: _____

_____

Answer: _____

**Clarification**

Word 1: _____

Definition: _____

_____

_____

Word 2: _____

Definition: _____

_____

**Summarization**

Whom or what: _____

Most important thing: _____

_____

Main idea:

_____ _____ _____ _____

_____ _____ _____ _____

_____ _____ _____ _____

_____ _____ _____ _____

**Passage Selected**

Page number: _____

Comments about passage: _____

_____

_____

_____

_____

_____

_____

# Fluency Practice: Information Learned

Name _____ Date _____

# Hatchet

It was still very early, only just past true dawn, and the water was so calm he could see his reflection. It frightened him—the face was cut and bleeding—swollen and lumpy, the hair all matted, and on his forehead a cut had healed but left the hair stuck with blood and scab. His eyes were slits in the bites and he was—somehow—covered with dirt. He slapped the water with his hand to destroy the mirror.

Ugly, he thought. Very, very ugly.

And he was, at that moment, almost overcome with self-pity. He was dirty and starving and bitten and hurt and lonely and ugly and afraid and so completely miserable that it was like being in a pit, a dark, deep pit with no way out.

He sat back on the bank and fought crying. Then let it come and cried for perhaps three, four minutes. Long tears, self-pity tears, wasted tears.

He stood, went back to the water, and took small drinks. As soon as the cold water hit his stomach he felt the hunger sharpen, as it had before, and he stood and held his abdomen until the hunger cramps receded.

He had to eat. He was weak with it again, down with the hunger, and he had to eat.

Back at the shelter the berries lay in a pile where he had dumped them when he grabbed his windbreaker—gut cherries he called them in his mind now—and he thought of eating some of them. Not such a crazy amount, as he had, which he felt brought on the sickness in the night—but just enough to stave off the hunger a bit.

He crawled into the shelter. Some flies were on the berries and he brushed them off. He selected only the berries that were solidly ripe—not the light red ones, but the berries that were dark, maroon red to black and swollen in ripeness. When he had a small handful of them he went back down to the lake and washed them in the water—small fish scattered away when he splashed the water up and he wished he had a fishing line and hook—then he ate them carefully, spitting out the pits. They were still tart, but had a sweetness to them, although they seemed to make his lips a bit numb.

When he finished he was still hungry, but the edge was gone and his legs didn't feel as weak as they had.

**Directions: Write three things you learned after reading the fluency passage.**

**1.** I learned _____

_____.

**2.** I learned _____

_____.

**3.** I learned _____

_____.

**Lesson**

**5**

# Think-Pair-Share

Name _____ Date _____

**Create**

*Create* a journal entry you think Brian would write in response to the prompt, "What I did on my summer vacation. . . ." Include specifics about what happened to Brian, as if it happened to you.

**Lesson 1**

Book Title _____

# Reciprocal-Teaching Chart

Name _____ Date _____

**Group Members:**

Discussion Leader/Passage Selector _____  Predictor/Character Analyzer _____

Question Generator _____  Clarifier _____  Summarizer _____

| **Prediction of Excerpt** | **Character Analysis** |
|---|---|
| _____ | Character details: _____ |
| _____ | _____ |
| _____ | _____ |
| _____ | Personal connections: _____ |
| **Verification** | _____ |
| | _____ |
| CORRECT     INCORRECT | _____ |

| **Question Generation** | **Clarification** |
|---|---|
| Literal question: _____ | Word 1: _____ |
| _____ | Definition: _____ |
| Answer: _____ | _____ |
| _____ | _____ |
| Inferential question: _____ | Word 2: _____ |
| _____ | Definition: _____ |
| Answer: _____ | _____ |

| **Summarization** | **Passage Selected** |
|---|---|
| Whom or what: _____ | Page number: _____ |
| Most important thing: _____ | Comments about passage: _____ |
| _____ | _____ |
| Main idea: | _____ |
| ____  ____  ____  ____ | _____ |
| ____  ____  ____  ____ | _____ |
| ____  ____  ____  ____ | _____ |
| ____  ____  ____  ____ | _____ |

## Lesson 2

Book Title _____

# Reciprocal-Teaching Chart

Name _____ Date _____

**Group Members:**

Discussion Leader/Passage Selector _____    Predictor/Character Analyzer _____

Question Generator _____    Clarifier _____    Summarizer _____

### Prediction of Excerpt

_____

_____

_____

_____

### Verification

CORRECT      INCORRECT

### Question Generation

Literal question: _____

_____

Answer: _____

_____

Inferential question: _____

_____

Answer: _____

### Summarization

Whom or what: _____

Most important thing: _____

_____

Main idea:

_____

_____

_____

_____

### Character Analysis

Character details: _____

_____

_____

Personal connections: _____

_____

_____

_____

### Clarification

Word 1: _____

Definition: _____

_____

_____

Word 2: _____

Definition: _____

_____

### Passage Selected

Page number: _____

Comments about passage: _____

_____

_____

_____

_____

## Lesson 2

# Fluency Practice: Mental Imagery

Name _____ Date _____

## Hatchet

There were these things to do.

He transferred all the eggs from the small beach into the shelter, reburying them near his sleeping area. It took all his will to keep from eating another one as he moved them, but he got it done and when they were out of sight again it was easier. He added wood to the fire and cleaned up the camp area.

A good laugh, that—cleaning up the camp. All he did was shake out his windbreaker and hang it in the sun to dry the berry juice that had soaked in, and smooth the sand where he slept.

But it was a mental thing. He had gotten depressed thinking about how they hadn't found him yet, and when he was busy and had something to do the depression seemed to leave.

So there were things to do.

With the camp squared away he brought in more wood. He had decided to always have enough on hand for three days and after spending one night with the fire for a friend he knew what a staggering amount of wood it would take. He worked all through the morning at the wood, breaking down dead limbs and breaking or chopping them in smaller pieces, storing them neatly beneath the overhang. He stopped once to take a drink at the lake and in his reflection he saw that the swelling on his head was nearly gone. There was no pain there so he assumed that had taken care of itself. His leg was also back to normal, although he had a small pattern of holes—roughly star-shaped— where the quills had nailed him, and while he was standing at the lake shore taking stock he noticed that his body was changing.

He had never been fat, but he had been slightly heavy with a little extra weight just above his belt at the sides.

This was completely gone and his stomach had caved in to the hunger and the sun had cooked him past burning so he was tanning, and with the smoke from the fire his face was starting to look like leather. But perhaps more than his body was the change in his mind, or in the way he was—was becoming.

I am not the same, he thought. I see, I hear differently.

• • • • • • • • • • • • • • • • • • • • • • • • • • • • • • • • • • • • •

**Directions: Illustrate what you thought about.**

**Lesson 3**

Book Title _____

# Reciprocal-Teaching Chart

Name _____ Date _____

**Group Members:**

Discussion Leader/Passage Selector _____

Predictor/Character Analyzer _____

Question Generator _____ Clarifier _____ Summarizer _____

| **Prediction of Excerpt** | **Character Analysis** |
|---|---|
| _____ | Character details: _____ |
| _____ | _____ |
| _____ | _____ |
| _____ | Personal connections: _____ |
| **Verification** | _____ |
| CORRECT    INCORRECT | _____ |
| | _____ |

| **Question Generation** | **Clarification** |
|---|---|
| Literal question: _____ | Word 1: _____ |
| _____ | Definition: _____ |
| Answer: _____ | _____ |
| _____ | _____ |
| Inferential question: _____ | Word 2: _____ |
| _____ | Definition: _____ |
| Answer: _____ | _____ |

| **Summarization** | **Passage Selected** |
|---|---|
| Whom or what: _____ | Page number: _____ |
| Most important thing: _____ | Comments about passage: _____ |
| _____ | _____ |
| Main idea: | _____ |
| _____ _____ _____ _____ | _____ |
| _____ _____ _____ _____ | _____ |
| _____ _____ _____ _____ | _____ |
| _____ _____ _____ _____ | _____ |

**Lesson 3**

# Fluency Practice: Standardized Test

Name _____ Date _____

## Hatchet

There were these things to do.

He transferred all the eggs from the small beach into the shelter, reburying them near his sleeping area. It took all his will to keep from eating another one as he moved them, but he got it done and when they were out of sight again it was easier. He added wood to the fire and cleaned up the camp area.

A good laugh, that—cleaning up the camp. All he did was shake out his windbreaker and hang it in the sun to dry the berry juice that had soaked in, and smooth the sand where he slept.

But it was a mental thing. He had gotten depressed thinking about how they hadn't found him yet, and when he was busy and had something to do the depression seemed to leave.

So there were things to do.

With the camp squared away he brought in more wood. He had decided to always have enough on hand for three days and after spending one night with the fire for a friend he knew what a staggering amount of wood it would take. He worked all through the morning at the wood, breaking down dead limbs and breaking or chopping them in smaller pieces, storing them neatly beneath the overhang. He stopped once to take a drink at the lake and in his reflection he saw that the swelling on his head was nearly gone. There was no pain there so he assumed that had taken care of itself. His leg was also back to normal, although he had a small pattern of holes—roughly star-shaped—where the quills had nailed him, and while he was standing at the lake shore taking stock he noticed that his body was changing.

He had never been fat, but he had been slightly heavy with a little extra weight just above his belt at the sides.

This was completely gone and his stomach had caved in to the hunger and the sun had cooked him past burning so he was tanning, and with the smoke from the fire his face was starting to look like leather. But perhaps more than his body was the change in his mind, or in the way he was—was becoming.

I am not the same, he thought. I see, I hear differently.

Score _____ /8 = _____ %

**Directions: Take turns reading the questions. Answer the questions together.**

**Level 1:** "Remember" Questions—each worth 1 point

**For Level 1 questions, fill in the space next to the correct answer in your own Workbook.**

**1.** What did Brian transfer from the small beach back to his shelter?

- ○ a. Eggs
- ○ b. Water
- ○ c. Fish
- ○ d. Roots

# Fluency Practice: Standardized Test, continued

Name _____ Date _____

2. How did Brian clean up his camp area?
   ○ a. He put all the extra food near his shelter and burned his garbage in the fire.
   ○ b. He removed big rocks and pulled weeds around where he slept.
   ○ c. He hung his windbreaker in the sun and smoothed the sand where he slept.
   ○ d. He piled all the firewood in one area and swept away extra debris with his hand.

3. Why did Brian try to keep busy?
   ○ a. He didn't want to think about how hungry he was.
   ○ b. Keeping busy helped him feel less lonely.
   ○ c. He had a lot of time to fill, being alone in the wilderness.
   ○ d. He had gotten depressed thinking about how he hadn't been rescued.

4. What did Brian do after he "squared away" his camp area?
   ○ a. He took a nap.                    ○ c. He looked for more food.
   ○ b. He brought in more wood.          ○ d. He went swimming in the lake.

> **Level 2:** "Understand" Questions—worth 2 points (2 points for correct answer, 1 point for partially correct answer, 0 points for incorrect answer)

**For the Level 2 questions, write the answer in the spaces provided in your own Workbook.**

5. Explain how Brian's body was healing. _____

_____

_____

_____

_____

_____

6. Explain how Brian's body was changing. _____

_____

_____

_____

_____

_____

_____

**Lesson 4**

Book Title _____

# Reciprocal-Teaching Chart

Name _____ Date _____

**Group Members:**

_____
Discussion Leader/Passage Selector

_____
Predictor/Character Analyzer

_____
Question Generator

_____
Clarifier

_____
Summarizer

| **Prediction of Excerpt** | **Character Analysis** |
|---|---|
| _____ | Character details: _____ |
| _____ | _____ |
| _____ | _____ |
| _____ | Personal connections: _____ |
| **Verification** | _____ |
| | _____ |
| CORRECT    INCORRECT | _____ |
| | _____ |

| **Question Generation** | **Clarification** |
|---|---|
| Literal question: _____ | Word 1: _____ |
| _____ | Definition: _____ |
| Answer: _____ | _____ |
| _____ | _____ |
| Inferential question: _____ | Word 2: _____ |
| _____ | Definition: _____ |
| Answer: _____ | _____ |

| **Summarization** | **Passage Selected** |
|---|---|
| Whom or what: _____ | Page number: _____ |
| Most important thing: _____ | Comments about passage: _____ |
| | _____ |
| Main idea: | _____ |
| _____  _____  _____ | _____ |
| _____  _____  _____ | _____ |
| _____  _____  _____ | _____ |
| _____  _____  _____. | _____ |

## Lesson 4

# Fluency Practice: Information Learned

Name _____ Date _____

## Hatchet

There were these things to do.

He transferred all the eggs from the small beach into the shelter, reburying them near his sleeping area. It took all his will to keep from eating another one as he moved them, but he got it done and when they were out of sight again it was easier. He added wood to the fire and cleaned up the camp area.

A good laugh, that—cleaning up the camp. All he did was shake out his windbreaker and hang it in the sun to dry the berry juice that had soaked in, and smooth the sand where he slept.

But it was a mental thing. He had gotten depressed thinking about how they hadn't found him yet, and when he was busy and had something to do the depression seemed to leave.

So there were things to do.

With the camp squared away he brought in more wood. He had decided to always have enough on hand for three days and after spending one night with the fire for a friend he knew what a staggering amount of wood it would take. He worked all through the morning at the wood, breaking down dead limbs and breaking or chopping them in smaller pieces, storing them neatly beneath the overhang. He stopped once to take a drink at the lake and in his reflection he saw that the swelling on his head was nearly gone. There was no pain there so he assumed that had taken care of itself. His leg was also back to normal, although he had a small pattern of holes—roughly star-shaped— where the quills had nailed him, and while he was standing at the lake shore taking stock he noticed that his body was changing.

He had never been fat, but he had been slightly heavy with a little extra weight just above his belt at the sides.

This was completely gone and his stomach had caved in to the hunger and the sun had cooked him past burning so he was tanning, and with the smoke from the fire his face was starting to look like leather. But perhaps more than his body was the change in his mind, or in the way he was—was becoming.

I am not the same, he thought. I see, I hear differently.

· · · · · · · · · · · · · · · · · · · · · · · · · · · · · · · · · · · · · · · · · · ·

**Directions: Write three things you learned after reading the fluency passage.**

**1.** I learned _____

_____.

**2.** I learned _____

_____.

**3.** I learned _____

_____.

## Think-Pair-Share

Name _____ Date _____

**Directions**

**Use the Think-Pair-Share Strategy to complete the question below.**

**Step 1:** **Think** about the question for one minute.

**Step 2:** **Pair,** and complete the question with your partner.

**Step 3:** **Share** what you wrote with the class.

· · · · · · · · · · · · · · · · · · · · · · · · · · · · · · · · · · · · · · · · · · · · · · · · ·

**Create**

*Create* a menu of the foods you think Brian would love to choose from upon being rescued.

Lesson 1

Book Title _____

# Reciprocal-Teaching Chart

Name _____ Date _____

**Group Members:**

Discussion Leader/Passage Selector _____ Predictor/Character Analyzer _____

Question Generator _____ Clarifier _____ Summarizer _____

| **Prediction of Excerpt** | **Character Analysis** |
|---|---|
| _____ | Character details: _____ |
| _____ | _____ |
| _____ | _____ |
| _____ | Personal connections: _____ |
| **Verification** | _____ |
| | _____ |
| CORRECT    INCORRECT | _____ |
| | _____ |
| **Question Generation** | **Clarification** |
| Literal question: _____ | Word 1: _____ |
| _____ | Definition: _____ |
| Answer: _____ | _____ |
| _____ | _____ |
| Inferential question: _____ | Word 2: _____ |
| _____ | Definition: _____ |
| Answer: _____ | _____ |
| **Summarization** | **Passage Selected** |
| Whom or what: _____ | Page number: _____ |
| Most important thing: _____ | Comments about passage: _____ |
| _____ | _____ |
| Main idea: | _____ |
| ____ ____ ____ | _____ |
| ____ ____ ____ | _____ |
| ____ ____ ____ | _____ |
| ____ ____ ____ | _____ |

**Lesson 2**

Book Title _____

# Reciprocal-Teaching Chart

Name _____ Date _____

**Group Members:**

_____     _____
Discussion Leader/Passage Selector          Predictor/Character Analyzer

_____     _____     _____
Question Generator                    Clarifier                         Summarizer

| **Prediction of Excerpt** | **Character Analysis** |
|---|---|
| _____ | Character details: _____ |
| _____ | _____ |
| _____ | _____ |
| _____ | Personal connections: _____ |
| **Verification** | _____ |
| | _____ |
| CORRECT      INCORRECT | _____ |
| | _____ |

| **Question Generation** | **Clarification** |
|---|---|
| Literal question: _____ | Word 1: _____ |
| _____ | Definition: _____ |
| Answer: _____ | _____ |
| _____ | _____ |
| Inferential question: _____ | Word 2: _____ |
| _____ | Definition: _____ |
| Answer: _____ | _____ |

| **Summarization** | **Passage Selected** |
|---|---|
| Whom or what: _____ | Page number: _____ |
| Most important thing: _____ | Comments about passage: _____ |
| _____ | _____ |
| Main idea: | _____ |
| _____ | _____ |
| _____ | _____ |
| _____ | _____ |
| _____ | _____ |

## Lesson 2

# Fluency Practice: Mental Imagery

Name _____ Date_____

## Hatchet

And now he stood at the end of the long part of the lake and was not the same, would not be the same again.

There had been many First Days.

First Arrow Day—when he had used thread from his tattered old piece of windbreaker and some pitch from a stump to put slivers of feather on a dry willow shaft and make an arrow that would fly correctly. Not accurately—he never got really good with it—but fly correctly so that if a rabbit or a foolbird sat in one place long enough, close enough, and he had enough arrows, he could hit it.

That brought First Rabbit Day—when he killed one of the large rabbits with an arrow and skinned it as he had the first bird, cooked it the same to find the meat as good—not as rich as the bird, but still good—and there were strips of fat on the back of the rabbit that cooked into the meat to make it richer.

Now he went back and forth between rabbits and foolbirds when he could, filling in with fish in the middle.

Always hungry.

I am always hungry but I can do it now, I can get food and I know I can get food and it makes me more. I know what I can do.

He moved closer to the lake to a stand of nut brush. These were thick bushes with little stickler pods that held green nuts—nuts that he thought he might be able to eat but they weren't ripe yet. He was out for a foolbird and they liked to hide in the base of the thick part of the nut brush, back in where the stems were close together and provided cover.

In the second clump he saw a bird, moved close to it, paused when the head feathers came up and it made a sound like a cricket—a sign of alarm just before it flew—then moved closer when the feathers went down and the bird relaxed. He did this four times, never looking at the bird directly, moving toward it at an angle so that it seemed he was moving off to the side—he had perfected this method after many attempts and it worked so well that he had actually caught one with his bare hands—until he was standing less than three feet from the bird, which was frozen in a hiding attitude in the brush.

**Directions: Illustrate what you thought about.**

**Lesson 3**

Book Title _____

# Reciprocal-Teaching Chart

Name _____ Date _____

**Group Members:**

Discussion Leader/Passage Selector _____  Predictor/Character Analyzer _____

Question Generator _____  Clarifier _____  Summarizer _____

| **Prediction of Excerpt** | **Character Analysis** |
|---|---|
| _____ | Character details: _____ |
| _____ | _____ |
| _____ | _____ |
| _____ | Personal connections: _____ |
| | _____ |
| **Verification** | _____ |
| | _____ |
| CORRECT     INCORRECT | _____ |

| **Question Generation** | **Clarification** |
|---|---|
| Literal question: _____ | Word 1: _____ |
| _____ | Definition: _____ |
| Answer: _____ | _____ |
| _____ | _____ |
| Inferential question: _____ | Word 2: _____ |
| _____ | Definition: _____ |
| Answer: _____ | _____ |

| **Summarization** | **Passage Selected** |
|---|---|
| Whom or what: _____ | Page number: _____ |
| Most important thing: _____ | Comments about passage: _____ |
| _____ | _____ |
| Main idea: | _____ |
| _____ | _____ |
| _____ | _____ |
| _____ | _____ |
| _____ | _____ |

# Fluency Practice: Standardized Test

Name _____ Date _____

## Hatchet

And now he stood at the end of the long part of the lake and was not the same, would not be the same again.

There had been many First Days.

First Arrow Day—when he had used thread from his tattered old piece of windbreaker and some pitch from a stump to put slivers of feather on a dry willow shaft and make an arrow that would fly correctly. Not accurately—he never got really good with it—but fly correctly so that if a rabbit or a foolbird sat in one place long enough, close enough, and he had enough arrows, he could hit it.

That brought First Rabbit Day—when he killed one of the large rabbits with an arrow and skinned it as he had the first bird, cooked it the same to find the meat as good—not as rich as the bird, but still good—and there were strips of fat on the back of the rabbit that cooked into the meat to make it richer.

Now he went back and forth between rabbits and foolbirds when he could, filling in with fish in the middle.

Always hungry.

I am always hungry but I can do it now, I can get food and I know I can get food and it makes me more. I know what I can do.

He moved closer to the lake to a stand of nut brush. These were thick bushes with little stickler pods that held green nuts—nuts that he thought he might be able to eat but they weren't ripe yet. He was out for a foolbird and they liked to hide in the base of the thick part of the nut brush, back in where the stems were close together and provided cover.

In the second clump he saw a bird, moved close to it, paused when the head feathers came up and it made a sound like a cricket—a sign of alarm just before it flew—then moved closer when the feathers went down and the bird relaxed. He did this four times, never looking at the bird directly, moving toward it at an angle so that it seemed he was moving off to the side—he had perfected this method after many attempts and it worked so well that he had actually caught one with his bare hands—until he was standing less than three feet from the bird, which was frozen in a hiding attitude in the brush.

Score _____ /8 = _____ %

**Directions: Take turns reading the questions. Answer the questions together.**

**Level 1:** "Remember" Questions—each worth 1 point

**For Level 1 questions, fill in the space next to the correct answer in your own Workbook.**

**1.** Which type of tree did Brian use to make arrows?
  ○ a. Maple          ○ c. Willow
  ○ b. Oak            ○ d. Birch

**Lesson 3**

# Fluency Practice: Standardized Test, continued

Name _____ Date _____

**2.** What was First Arrow Day?
- ○ a. The day Brian found the first of many old arrowheads.
- ○ b. The day Brian first attempted to go hunting.
- ○ c. The day Brian successfully hunted and killed wild game with an arrow.
- ○ d. The day Brian made an arrow that would fly correctly.

**3.** What was First Rabbit Day?
- ○ a. The day Brian killed a large rabbit.
- ○ b. The day Brian first tried to trap a large rabbit.
- ○ c. The day Brian discovered the first rabbit hole.
- ○ d. The day Brian hunted and caught a large rabbit with his bare hands.

**4.** What did Brian eat when he was not able to catch rabbits or foolbirds?
- ○ a. Nuts
- ○ c. Fish
- ○ b. Eggs
- ○ d. Berries

---

**Level 2:** "Understand" Questions—worth 2 points (2 points for correct answer, 1 point for partially correct answer, 0 points for incorrect answer)

---

**For the Level 2 questions, write the answer in the spaces provided in your own Workbook.**

**5.** Explain where Brian hunted foolbirds and why he knew to hunt there. _____

_____

_____

_____

_____

_____

**6.** Explain Brian's technique for hunting a foolbird. _____

_____

_____

_____

_____

_____

## Lesson 4

Book Title _____

# Reciprocal-Teaching Chart

Name _____ Date _____

**Group Members:**

Discussion Leader/Passage Selector _____  Predictor/Character Analyzer _____

Question Generator _____  Clarifier _____  Summarizer _____

### Prediction of Excerpt

_____

_____

_____

### Verification

CORRECT        INCORRECT

### Question Generation

Literal question: _____

_____

Answer: _____

_____

Inferential question: _____

_____

Answer: _____

### Summarization

Whom or what: _____

Most important thing: _____

_____

Main idea:

_____    _____

_____    _____

_____    _____

_____    _____.

### Character Analysis

Character details: _____

_____

Personal connections: _____

_____

_____

_____

### Clarification

Word 1: _____

Definition: _____

_____

_____

Word 2: _____

Definition: _____

### Passage Selected

Page number: _____

Comments about passage: _____

_____

_____

_____

_____

_____

## End-of-Book Reciprocal-Teaching Chart

Name _____ Date _____

**Group Members:**

_____

Discussion Leader/Passage Selector          Predictor/Character Analyzer

_____

Question Generator                          Clarifier

_____

Summarizer

| | |
|---|---|
| **Author(s)** | **Genre** |
| _____ | ☐ Fiction  ☐ Nonfiction |
| | **Theme** |
| | What is the moral of the story? |
| **Illustrator(s) (if any)** | |
| _____ | _____ |
| | _____ |
| **Author's Purpose:** | **Perspective** |
| Why did the author(s) write the story? | What is the point of view of the story? |
| ☐ To persuade  ☐ To inform  ☐ To entertain | ☐ First person  ☐ Second person |
| | ☐ Third person |
| **Mood** | **Conflict:** _____ |
| How did you feel while you read the story? | _____ |
| _____ | _____ |
| _____ | **Climax:** _____ |
| _____ | _____ |
| _____ | _____ |
| _____ | **Resolution:** _____ |
| _____ | _____ |
| _____ | _____ |
| _____ | _____ |

# Fluency Practice: Information Learned

Name _____ Date_____

## Hatchet

And now he stood at the end of the long part of the lake and was not the same, would not be the same again.

There had been many First Days.

First Arrow Day—when he had used thread from his tattered old piece of windbreaker and some pitch from a stump to put slivers of feather on a dry willow shaft and make an arrow that would fly correctly. Not accurately—he never got really good with it—but fly correctly so that if a rabbit or a foolbird sat in one place long enough, close enough, and he had enough arrows, he could hit it.

That brought First Rabbit Day—when he killed one of the large rabbits with an arrow and skinned it as he had the first bird, cooked it the same to find the meat as good—not as rich as the bird, but still good—and there were strips of fat on the back of the rabbit that cooked into the meat to make it richer.

Now he went back and forth between rabbits and foolbirds when he could, filling in with fish in the middle.

Always hungry.

I am always hungry but I can do it now, I can get food and I know I can get food and it makes me more. I know what I can do.

He moved closer to the lake to a stand of nut brush. These were thick bushes with little stickler pods that held green nuts—nuts that he thought he might be able to eat but they weren't ripe yet. He was out for a foolbird and they liked to hide in the base of the thick part of the nut brush, back in where the stems were close together and provided cover.

In the second clump he saw a bird, moved close to it, paused when the head feathers came up and it made a sound like a cricket—a sign of alarm just before it flew—then moved closer when the feathers went down and the bird relaxed. He did this four times, never looking at the bird directly, moving toward it at an angle so that it seemed he was moving off to the side—he had perfected this method after many attempts and it worked so well that he had actually caught one with his bare hands—until he was standing less than three feet from the bird, which was frozen in a hiding attitude in the brush.

**Directions: Write three things you learned after reading the fluency passage.**

1. I learned _____

_____.

2. I learned _____

_____.

3. I learned _____

_____.

## Lesson 5

# Think-Pair-Share

Name _____ Date _____

**Use the Think-Pair-Share Strategy to complete the question below.**

**Step 1:** **Think** about the question for one minute.

**Step 2:** **Pair,** and complete the question with your partner.

**Step 3:** **Share** what you wrote with the class.

. . . . . . . . . . . . . . . . . . . . . . . . . . . . . . . . . . . . . . . . . . . .

**Create**

Specific events in Gary Paulsen's life gave him the knowledge to write *Hatchet*. *Create* a book report that explains how Paulsen's research and life experiences helped him write a better book.

## Scoring

| 6 Traits of Writing (and their characteristics) | 1 point Beginning (No characteristics present.) | 2 points Emerging (Some characteristics present.) | 3 points Developing (About half of characteristics present.) | 4 points Proficient (Most characteristics present.) | 5 points (maximum possible) Strong (Characteristics all present.) | 6 points (bonus) Exemplary |
|---|---|---|---|---|---|---|
| **Ideas** Descriptions and details are well developed, informative, and related to the topic, and they get the reader interested. | | | | | | |
| **Organization** Paper is correct length; contains title page with title, name, and date; has thoughtful transitions; uses logical sequencing; has summary. | | | | | | |
| **Voice** Writing style is engaging, with active voice, making the reader want to read on to learn more. | | | | | | |
| **Word Choice** Word choice is varied, complex, and interesting, allowing the reader to become interested in the story. | | | | | | |
| **Sentence Fluency** Writing is smooth and easy to read, with varied sentence structure. | | | | | | |
| **Conventions** Correct grammar, punctuation, spelling, paragraphing, and capitalization are evident. | | | | | | |

# Fluency Chart

Name _____

| | Unit | 1 | 2 | 3 | 4 | 5 | 6 | 7 | 8 | 9 | 10 | 11 | 12 | 13 | 14 | 15 |
|---|---|---|---|---|---|---|---|---|---|---|---|---|---|---|---|---|
| | 300 | | | | | | | | | | | | | | | |
| | 290 | | | | | | | | | | | | | | | |
| | 280 | | | | | | | | | | | | | | | |
| | 270 | | | | | | | | | | | | | | | |
| | 260 | | | | | | | | | | | | | | | |
| | 250 | | | | | | | | | | | | | | | |
| | 240 | | | | | | | | | | | | | | | |
| | 230 | | | | | | | | | | | | | | | |
| | 220 | | | | | | | | | | | | | | | |
| | 210 | | | | | | | | | | | | | | | |
| | 200 | | | | | | | | | | | | | | | |
| | 190 | | | | | | | | | | | | | | | |
| | 180 | | | | | | | | | | | | | | | |
| | 170 | | | | | | | | | | | | | | | |
| | 160 | | | | | | | | | | | | | | | |
| | 150 | | | | | | | | | | | | | | | |
| | 140 | | | | | | | | | | | | | | | |
| | 130 | | | | | | | | | | | | | | | |
| | 120 | | | | | | | | | | | | | | | |
| | 110 | | | | | | | | | | | | | | | |
| | 100 | | | | | | | | | | | | | | | |
| | 90 | | | | | | | | | | | | | | | |
| | 80 | | | | | | | | | | | | | | | |
| | 70 | | | | | | | | | | | | | | | |
| | 60 | | | | | | | | | | | | | | | |
| | 50 | | | | | | | | | | | | | | | |
| | 40 | | | | | | | | | | | | | | | |
| | 30 | | | | | | | | | | | | | | | |
| | 20 | | | | | | | | | | | | | | | |
| | 10 | | | | | | | | | | | | | | | |
| | 0 | | | | | | | | | | | | | | | |

| Unit | 1 | 2 | 3 | 4 | 5 | 6 | 7 | 8 | 9 | 10 | 11 | 12 | 13 | 14 | 15 |
|---|---|---|---|---|---|---|---|---|---|---|---|---|---|---|---|
| CWPM— Cold | | | | | | | | | | | | | | | |
| CWPM— Hot | | | | | | | | | | | | | | | |
| Did I Improve? | Yes No | Yes No | Yes No | Yes No | Yes No | Yes No | Yes No | Yes No | Yes No | Yes No | Yes No | Yes No | Yes No | Yes No | Yes No |
| Did I Meet/Exceed Goal Line? | Yes No | Yes No | Yes No | Yes No | Yes No | Yes No | Yes No | Yes No | Yes No | Yes No | Yes No | Yes No | Yes No | Yes No | Yes No |

———— = 50th percentile (150 CWPM)    ———— = 75th percentile (177 CWPM)    ———— = 90th percentile (202 CWPM)